READY, SET, GRIT

Ready, Set, Grit

The information given in this book should not be treated as a substitute for professional medical advice. Always consult a medical practitioner.

Although every effort has been made to ensure that the information in this book was correct at press time, no responsibility is assumed for any loss, damage, or disruption caused by errors or omissions and no liability is assumed for any damaged that may result from the use of this information.

The views expressed in this book are those of the author alone and do not necessary reflect those of That Guy's House.

This book is a work of nonfiction, however, certain elements may have been fictionalized to suit the narrative.

The book information is catalogued as follows;

Author Name(s): Elin Barton

Title: Ready, Set, Grit

Description; First Edition

1st Edition, YEAR

Book Design by Madison Tinney

ISBN 978-1-913479-95-4

ISBN (ebook) 978-1-913479-96-1

Published by That Guy's House

www.ThatGuysHouse.com

READY

THREE STEPS TO SUCCESS IN LIFE, BUSINESS AND THE PURSUIT OF HAPPINESS

SET GRIT

Elin Barton

PRAISE FOR READY, SET, GRIT

"With passion and purpose, *Ready, Set, Grit* leads the reader on a riveting journey beyond one's wildest imagination. Through the process, powerful tools to amplify success will propel you to be the most incredible version of yourself." - Laura Ponticello, best-selling author, *The Entrepreneurial Compass*

"*Ready, Set, Grit* can be summed up with "if you are still breathing it's not too late"! A great toolbox filled with "Power Tools" on how to get from where you are to where you want to go......... and once and for all REALLY figure out you do not have to do it alone!! Barton shares her journey in this enlightening read that takes you from preparation to the party! She says, "it's all fun and games in the rearview window" but to get there turn around and look thru the windshield and let her help you figure out where you are going.... enjoy the ride!" -Debbie Mrazek, author of *The Field Guide to Sales and CEO of The Sales Company*

"Are you being called to create the life you've always wanted? Those who dare step out of their comfort zone to create an "authentic life" would find it a solitary, uphill process, until now. Elin's approach to discovering one's "why" affords the reader a communal, "side-by-side" illustration of the discovery process in action with relatable examples throughout. If your "authentic you" is tugging at your sleeve, Ready, Set, Grit is your book." – Eric Uriarte, author of *The Zen Side of Business Ownership*

"In *Ready, Set, Grit* Elin offers a simple but often missed time tested framework for a successful life. It is satisfying to imagine the pleasure and the Aha! moments you the reader will have with each page you read, and the transformation of that whisper into a full-blown rumble." -Turk Akbay, best-selling author of *The #1 Habit-Make Your Life Easier and Reach Your Goals Faster*

"*Ready, Set, Grit* orients readers to the right, the sure, and the good in oneself! Elin Barton sets you on the path of soulful discovery and provides a foundation for new routes of relevance. To deconstruct and reconstruct 'success as meaning making' with a thought-provoking 'easy read' that invigorates self-catalytic actions for those dedicated to a necessary work 'in progress'." ~Violet Kashewa, *Business Psychic Expert*

*To all the kindred souls who refuse to believe
that life is ruled by limits or the status quo,
this one's for you.*

Contents

INTRODUCTION

Get Clear About What You Want, Why it's Important and How to Get It:

I recently wrote an article titled, "Make Each Day a Masterpiece."

Maybe it's hard, or impossible, even, to live up to that standard every single day, but I do want to look back on my life one day and know that I made a great adventure of it. That I did it on my terms, intentionally creating the parts of life that I most wanted – abundance, freedom, success, community, love, health and lots of laughter.

I believe that there are plenty of people who don't think about this kind of thing very often, but the danger with that is, you risk a life that happens "to you" rather than one you intentionally design.

We all have the power within us to create the life we dream of, but all too often we talk ourselves out of achieving success before ever trying to grab it.

That's pretty messed up thinking, but people do it all the time. You know why? Because it's safer, and in some ways easier. But you have to admit, that path is also a lot less fun. And do you really want to get all the way to the end of your life without ever knowing what you could have done "if only..."?

I started a business twelve years ago and the life lessons that I've learned during those years far surpass the education I could have gotten anywhere else. This "school of hard knocks" did teach me about what's necessary to run and sustain a business. Perhaps most importantly, I learned that the first step to achieving anything at all is to look inward and deal with your own baggage.

I wanted to understand how to be successful, so I started searching for both answers and mentors. At any opportunity I would try to talk with or interview successful people to try to figure out what their secret sauce was. What I discovered are three main components which are the tenets around which this book is constructed.

In the first section, "Ready", we'll explore mindset and purpose. Then, in the second, "Set", we'll look at your foundational elements – time, money and tribe. And finally, the last section, "Grit", outlines a plan for actually doing the work. We'll also look at the importance of celebrating successes and milestones - not someday, but NOW.

There are a lot of books out there that are designed to help people navigate both business and life, and I'm honored that you've chosen to share your journey with me. My intention is that this book will help you get clear about what you want, why it's important and how to achieve those goals.

Because being supported by a powerful community is a critical part of the journey, I invite you to join our online community and connect with other like-minded entrepreneurs at theboardroom.elinbarton.com.

Being willing to step out of your comfort zone, while becoming more intentional and making meaningful changes are actions that most people won't ever bother with. Deciding to change is the first step, and since you've read this far, I'm guessing that you're one of the special ones who's ready to take a chance and to start making a real difference for yourself and those around you.

Let's do this. Buckle up, dig in and get ready for the ride of your life, because YOU are worth it.

PART 1
READY

Get ready to lay a solid foundation for your future. In the following pages, you'll learn about the importance of creating a clear vision and for taming the old, limiting beliefs that no longer serve you.
But before you can build, first you must learn to listen to the most important voice of them all...

CHAPTER 1
THE VOICE

Your time is limited, so don't waste it living someone
else's life. Don't be trapped by dogma - which is living
with the results of other people's thinking.
Don't let the noise of others' opinions drown out your
own inner voice. And most important, have the courage
to follow your heart and intuition.
- **Steve Jobs**

Have you ever heard the rumblings of your soul?

Maybe it begins as more of a whisper than a rumble, but it's the kind of whisper that grabs your attention, if even for a fleeting moment. Perhaps you hear it when you're in the middle of doing the dishes or driving the kids to school. Or while you're in line checking out at the supermarket or at night when you're drifting off to sleep. This type of whisper can seductively appear at the most unexpected moments. You could be sitting in traffic, running on the treadmill or working on that big report for your boss.

The timing may catch you off guard, but this is different from your ordinary, run of the mill whisper. This one is the kind that infiltrates your thoughts, tugging at them insistently until they turn into full-on daydreams.

It draws you towards something and excites you, making your spine tingle. When you allow yourself to imagine the possibilities you feel joy, peace and a sense of belonging. This voice is not easily silenced, which tells you that the message is coming from deep within yourself. When you're quiet enough to hear it, you'll begin to be drawn into alignment with your life's purpose.

Kids are particularly skilled at hearing this voice, and at knowing – and acting upon – whatever will bring them joy in any particular moment. Whether they're inspired to put on a puppet show, build the world's most awesome Lego structure, or experiment with Mom's makeup, you need look no further than your average 5-year-old if you want to see someone who's following their bliss.

Yes, this quest for self-actualization can annoy the daylights out of the adults in the room, but there is so much we can learn from these pint-sized sages.

For example, a kid that age also wastes approximately zero seconds telling herself all the reasons she's not going to be good at something. Can she be a doctor? Adventurer? Chef? Movie star? Teacher? Undersea explorer? Of course she can! The world is full of endless possibilities and each of them is a source of joy, excitement and an opportunity to truly live solely and fully in the present moment.

So, am I suggesting that we all regress into our five-year-old brains?

Not really.

But kind of.

See, our adult brains tend to overthink things, putting oh-so-much-pressure on coming up with the "right" answer. We psych ourselves into believing that the stakes are so high that we have to "get it right" or risk unthinkable (and highly unpleasant) consequences. Forget about painting a picture for the fun of painting a picture. We either tell ourselves that we're horrible at painting or never give ourselves the opportunity to try.

The self-talk often goes something like this: "Our lives are very busy, and if we're going to spend our precious time painting a picture, then we'd better be good at it. We should be paid – or at least widely praised and admired."

This same principle stops us from doing any number of things.

Ignoring all of that self-talk and following your passion can lead to all kinds of interesting outcomes. As an added bonus you don't have to worry about one day being on your deathbed, saying, "Gosh, I wish I would have..." or "If only I'd been brave enough..."

Your passion doesn't necessarily have to become a business, but some of the world's most successful entities were started in this very way. Successful business leaders don't get caught up in worrying about what other people are going to think about their successes or failures. I recently saw Sir Richard Branson speak about his long, interesting and ultra-successful career. Never one to mince words, he shared that one of his tenets of success has been his commitment to this mantra: "Screw it, just do it."

That philosophy worked out splendidly for Sir Richard, and it will for you too. Don't get stuck in all the reasons something is not going to work out. Not ever trying in the first place is the only way you're ever really going to fail. There's more on failure in chapter four, so let's not go too far down that rabbit hole right now.

Instead let's keep our focus on developing your vision.

We already said that following your passion could become a business. It could also simply evolve into a fulfilling hobby or way to volunteer and give back to your community. The trick is to stop worrying about how you're going to achieve your goals.

Since knowing the step-by-step "how" of the way your dreams will come true is impossible, spending time worrying about this is a colossal waste of time.

You heard that correctly. You do not have to have everything figured out in advance, and you do not have to think through how you're going to navigate every bump on the road.

Let's get back to Sir Richard. If he had actually taken the time to think through all the reasons why starting a record company (or an airline or a spaceship company) were bound to fail, he could have easily talked himself out of taking the first step towards any of it. Instead, he didn't worry about what other people thought of him. He followed his instincts and his passion, worked his tail off, and had a lot of fun along the way.

The Importance of Getting Still

It's super easy to get distracted by day-to-day living and responsibilities. I'm not suggesting that you should walk away from your job, stop paying your bills or steadfastly ignore your kids or spouse in search of your bliss. You've got to continue to take care of business and pay attention to those who you care about. And at the same time, you've also got to give that voice of yours a seat at the table.

And that means actually taking time out to sit quietly with yourself. I know you're busy – everyone is. In fact, these days sometimes it feels like we're all part of a crazy competition where the most stressed out, busiest person wins the biggest and best badge of honor. The truth is, being busy isn't the same as being happy, satisfied and having a high quality of life.

Being too busy can create a buzz of activity that gives you an adrenaline rush. The problem is, when we're in that "busy mode" we don't hear our inner guidance very well at all. If we are unable to hear the inner voice, being busy becomes an easy excuse to fall back on and to talk ourselves out of taking any kind of action.

Do you answer your inner voice with any of the following brush-offs?

- *I'm too busy.*

- *I don't have enough money, time or resources to do that.*

- *I'm not good enough.*

- *I'll never be able to make that work.*

- *I'll embarrass myself.*

- *There are already so many people who are successful at this. What could I possibly contribute?*

If you recognize these excuses because you've used them, don't worry. The first step towards real and meaningful change is recognizing that you want and deserve something different.

Next, you've got to own the actions and thought patterns that have been keeping you stuck.

The Power of Intention

Let's face it, staying busy is easy.

Most of us never leave our jobs at the office because we carry them in our pockets and on our laptops. And even if we're not working, exactly, there are hundreds of distractions competing for our attention every single day. If you get caught in the trap of being busy without direction or intention, then it's probably not very difficult to imagine looking back in 10, 20, 30 or 40 years and wondering where all that time went.

That's why intentional creation of your life is so important. If you don't like your current circumstances, then stop pitching your tent there. When you step back and objectively look at your situation there is always something you can change or do differently, and your own inner voice will guide you there *if you're willing to listen to it.*

Hello? Is anybody in there?

Even if your inner voice has been feeling a little bit ignored lately, I promise you, it hasn't given up and gone away. Everyone has their own unique inner guidance system but most days we just don't pay attention. We've all been guilty of brushing our inspired thoughts aside as we navigate our day-to-day lives. We go to work, joke with our colleagues, grab a drink, watch TV, answer emails, pay the bills, pick up the kids, go to bed, wake up and do it all again the next day.

We spend countless hours doing things we aren't necessarily inspired by, but the thing about the soul is, it doesn't give up easily. And once you've noticed your own inner voice guiding you towards what you're really "supposed to be doing" it's very hard to un-hear it. It's a persistent thing, this voice. You'll feel its presence deeply, viscerally, on a cellular level.

Pressing the mute button on the voice, however, is a different story. It's possible – even easy – to ignore this calling of the soul for months, years or even a lifetime. And plenty of people do exactly that. In fact, based on all my research I happen to believe that most people do ignore it at one point or another.

Take Tasha, for example. Born into a family of lawyers, there was never much question about what she would end up doing with her life. In law school Tasha dutifully showed up and did the work even though she knew that her heart wasn't in it. The fear of disappointing her family was so great that she never spoke up. She made it through law school, passed the bar and landed a job with a reputable firm.

It took three more years of doing a job she hated to push Tasha to the breaking point. The moment of reckoning came when her doctor told her that her stress levels and blood pressure were through the roof. Tasha was scared and put in her notice that day. She had no idea what she was going to do with her life, but as it turns out walking away from the safe and predictable path was the best thing she ever did.

Tasha decided to help other stressed out professionals relax and reclaim their health and today she runs a successful spa and retreat center and has never been happier.

When Tasha was working at the law firm, she put the expectations of others above her own wishes and desires. And yes, sometimes in life your responsibilities require that you do have to prioritize paying the bills, but that doesn't mean it has to be your end game.

If You're Still Breathing, it's Not Too Late

As long as you're walking the earth you still have an opportunity to change and improve your circumstances. Do not let a temporary situation turn into an excuse not to pursue your dreams and your purpose.

Yes, meet your responsibilities. Paying the bills and taking care of your family is the right thing to do. But don't forget about your responsibility to yourself. You have an obligation to yourself to keep your dream alive and to figure out how to move the needle so you're closer to making that dream come true – even if you're only taking the very tiniest of baby steps.

Most people don't do this, of course. It's so much easier to accept the status quo. We're taught to check certain boxes, and to work to acquire certain things. Our biggest dreams and deepest desires often don't fit neatly into a box - which doesn't mean they're not important or that we can get away with not paying attention to them.

Of course, many people spend their whole lives never questioning any of it, never wondering about their true potential, or taking any steps toward testing the boundaries of all that's possible. Not paying attention is a choice. The truth is, you can never force someone else to chase a dream or explore their interests if they're not inclined to do so. The desire has to come from within. So, this isn't about someone else's dream. It's about yours.

The simple fact that you're reading this book already means you're not a status quo person. You're itching for something more and you want to find out how to get it. You know that life can be invigorating, fun and exciting. You understand that abundance, in all its forms, is something that is available to you if you just change the way you're doing a few things.

And besides, what if you actually looked forward to Mondays?

It sounds simple to tune into your own intuition or guidance system. However, in an age when there is so much noise from our devices, endless news and social media streams, and an ever revolving and expanding stable of talking heads, memes of the week, hashtag threads and other distractions, it can be challenging to get centered, quiet and tune into yourself.

Although carving out quiet time and space may require some effort on your part, it's totally worth it because that inner voice is everything. It's the sound of your soul talking. Your purpose. Your guiding light. Source. Allah. God. Whatever you call it, learning to hear what it has to say, and importantly, finding the courage to trust it and take action around that message, is probably one of the most important things you'll ever be called to do.

So, how do you do it? How do you learn to hear the voice and craft an action plan around what it's telling you? How do you differentiate the siren call of the soul from, say, effects of indigestion or of drinking too much wine?

You might feel inspired, but how do you know if your big idea is any good or whether it could possibly be turned into a business or life mission? And if your idea is solid, what if you don't have the resources to run with it, to start the business or to leave your day job? You may have a burning passion for writing, art or music but does that mean you can find a way to actually make money doing that thing that excites you?

What if your inner voice has ADHD and flits and flutters from one topic to the next like a butterfly in springtime?

Or, even worse, what if you don't hear any voice at all?

Believe me, your voice is there. And if you're alive and breathing then your work here on earth is not yet done. Still feeling skeptical? I'm going to ask you to come along with me and to do what countless coaches and teachers in both spiritual and business matters have requested of me over the years: trust the process.

> *You were put on this earth to achieve your greatest self,*
> *to live out your purpose, and to do it courageously.*
> - **Steve Maraboli, *Life, the Truth, and Being Free***

Let's start by playing a little game. If you think of life as a journey, where would you like to be in 20 years? 10? 5? What about in 6 months?

As you start painting the picture of what you want your life to look like it might be easy to fill in the blanks with tangible things. How many people have their own version of this vision: "I want a mansion by the sea, a garage full of sports cars, a life of glamour and travel."

Many people find that it's easy to list material things that they want, and to imagine the perceived freedom that money and financial security will bring them. But then what? What happens after you have the house and the cars and the lifestyle? Does that automatically mean you'll be happy? Does having free time mean you're fulfilled? You only need to look at any number of celebrities, especially those who skyrocketed very quickly to fame and fortune, to know that riches and happiness are not one and the same.

Early Retirement: And then What?

I talked to someone the other day who was very clear about what he wants. "I'm going to retire at age 40," he told me confidently. However, when I asked a few probing questions about why he wanted that and what he was going to do for fulfillment post-retirement, this young man quickly got to a point where he couldn't answer anymore. Although he had obviously thought about the topic a lot, he hadn't factored in that his fantasy life of leisure would become both lonely and kind of boring without the addition of some kind of purpose.

After our conversation he told me that he was heading back to the drawing board to fill in some of those important details. And you can do the same thing.

Part of living in the free world means that you get to define your own purpose. Every day you can hone your vision and decide what the most important components of your life vision are.

This is not a one-and-done process, either.

It's something that you'll do again and again because you're never really done working on yourself and your dreams. Achieve one goal and you'll replace it with another.

Retirement is a goal that many people view as the pinnacle of their careers – the moment they've been waiting their whole life for. For many people, however, a life of leisure is not what they imagined it would be. Without a purpose (or at least a project) many retirees become bored or depressed.

A lack of purpose can be so devastating in some retirees that there is a statistical spike in the death rate of retirees within the first two years following retirement. Researchers often attribute the increase in death rate to a declining social or economic position. The statistics can be sobering, but by no means is this to say that retirement is a deathtrap. On the contrary, retirement, like any other stage of life, is an opportunity to declare – and intentionally create – the life that you want.

Ever-Changing Goal Posts

Achieve something significant - landing your first job, making your first million dollars, knitting your first scarf – and you'll celebrate for a little while but then you can bet your bottom dollar that you're going to dream up some new goal. As humans we are designed to always be growing, learning and expanding, and when we're able to both hear and trust our inner guidance, we begin to navigate through life quicker, easier and more nimbly because we instinctively know what our next steps should be.

Ultimately, those steps will lead us closer to our own definition of success. Keep in mind that rarely does true and lasting happiness come from the attainment of houses, cars and other riches. There's nothing wrong with wanting (or having) material things, early retirement or a glamorous lifestyle, but if you're not also working on aligning with purpose you may find that true happiness and satisfaction remain elusive.

> *The purpose of our lives is to be happy.*
> **-Dalai Lama**

> *The purpose of life is a life of purpose.*
> **- Robert Bryne**

Let's go back to the core question of this chapter: What is it that you truly want?

Now let's frame that in terms of happiness and alignment with your purpose.

When you tap into that purpose and allow your natural gifts and awesomeness to shine, not only do you set yourself up to present your best self to the world, but it's also the place from which you can contribute the most to the greater good.

Let's face it – giving back feels good, and when you do step into the role that only you can play, that's when you begin to tap into a power that is greater than yourself. That's when real "life magic" begins, and what could possibly be more fun than that?

A word of caution: money in and of itself should not be your only end game. Because if it's just money you're seeking then there are plenty of high-paying, soul-sucking jobs that you can apply for. And if that truly is your biggest desire, I have no doubt that you'll be able to get hired into one of those positions by applying the principles in this book.

The Pursuit of Happiness

But will that truly lead to happiness? Only you know the answer to this question, but I would encourage you to make your own happiness a non-negotiable point as you design your dream life.

You can start working on your own happiness this very second. Make the decision to find happiness now. Not after you have the millions of dollars, ocean-side property and 1967 Corvette. Now. Today. Happiness is a choice and it can't be tied to the number in your bank account or whether the cashier at Starbucks is in a bad mood. Losses, hurts or disappointments may make you unhappy, of course. It's okay to be sad sometimes, but you don't have to stay in that emotional state forever.

At the end of the day, if you intentionally choose to travel through life focusing on wonder and joy you'll have a much different experience than someone who decides to stay stuck in looking at what's bad.

Unless you have a serious mental illness, you do have the choice to decide how to look at things in life, and in doing so you are intentionally creating the experience you're going to have.

While this book was written largely for people who are driven to turn their dream into a money-making venture, you certainly don't have to go that route. You can honor your inner voice by embracing a hobby or a volunteer position. You can figure out how to align your talents, your interests and your passions and channel that energy in the work that you already do. Or these new revelations might lead to you looking for a new job that is a better fit for your personality and interests.

The details of how it all plays out will ultimately be up to you, but taking the time to ask the questions and develop a plan around what you discover, then to actually carry out this plan, really can change the outcome of your entire life.

The Best of You

John left a high paying job in Manhattan to become a hairdresser in a small city in Upstate New York. He earns a decent living but it's just a fraction of what he used to make. Yet, he is living his purpose. He is one of the happiest people I know and always says that he feels like the luckiest person alive as he goes into work every day, doing a job he loves. No amount of money could lure him back to his old life in the city. He does work that excites him every single day and epitomizes someone whose life is in very strong alignment.

When you align with your purpose you end up giving the best of yourself to the world. By living an inspired, authentic life you create positive impacts for others, whether it's by giving direct help to someone who needs it or by setting an example for someone who may be inspired by your passion and your actions. Sometimes you know the people who you've helped, and other times you may never find out who you've impacted or how far your influence has truly spread. I promise, when you start really "walking your walk" people will notice. Your kids will pay attention (even if they pretend not to), as will your friends, colleagues and complete strangers. They may not articulate it to you directly, yet it will be there.

Even seemingly small changes in the way you're choosing to show up in the world can have a profound impact. You may have heard of the butterfly effect, which suggests that something which appears inconsequential – like the fluttering of a butterfly's wings – can ultimately have global impact. That's the same influence you can have when you commit to living in alignment with your life's purpose.

So, how do you do it?

How do you start hearing that Inner Voice and figuring out what your purpose (or Big Dream) is?

As many wise spiritual teachers have shared, the answers already lie within each of us; it's just a matter of learning to listen. Once you start tuning into your own inner voice it becomes easier and easier to hear. As with anything, practice is critical to ultimate success. So, consider incorporating a daily practice around getting in touch with your own intuition. The more you ask the questions and are open to receiving information and guidance, the easier the answers will flow. So, don't be afraid to flex those intuition muscles, and to trust in what they're telling you.

DAILY PRACTICE

- The first thing you'll want to do is to get into agreement with yourself that you're going to explore answers to your Big Questions without judgment. Be open to hearing your inner guidance and when you do, don't automatically start listing all the reasons why the thing it's telling you is impractical or impossible. Just observe, listen and trust.

- Next, make time to get still and start asking those Big Questions. These questions may include (but may not be limited to) exploring what it is that you really want out of life. You may not get the answer on the first day you try this.

Stick with it and dedicate some time – five to ten minutes a day – to sit quietly and contemplate this question.

In your dedicated time make sure your devices are off and that others know not to disturb you. Quiet your mind and begin to see yourself in your ideal future. Remember: no limitations. Don't worry about practical concerns. As you do this on a regular basis you'll start recognizing some revealing details. Most people eventually find the answers – or clues that will lead to answers – in one of three ways.

RSG Tip: It takes time to develop new habits and you may not know which method is right for you until you've done it repeatedly. Pick one method and try it every day for a week before moving onto the next one. That way you'll find what works best for you and you'll be able to settle into a daily practice.

Powerful Visualization. Close your eyes and imagine yourself in the future in a place where you're living your dream life. Imagine yourself already successful (let go of the details of how you got to this place). Let your future self be happy in this exercise and notice what it is you're doing, what people and things are around you, what kind of car you're driving and what kind of company you're working for or with. Don't worry about how you got to this place, and don't put any limits on what you let yourself see there.

Again, please silence your inner critic if you hear it say things like, "You can't afford that" or "You'll never be able to live in Paris. You don't even speak French!"

Just go with the flow and visualize. Set a timer for somewhere between 5-10 minutes, and when the timer goes off, you're done. Repeat the following day.

I Know What I DON'T Want. This is a game where you examine the different parts of your life and identify what it is that you don't want in each of them. You may not know what career you ultimately want to pursue but perhaps you know you don't want to work in a cubicle or in an office. You might not know where you want to live, but maybe you know in your heart of hearts that wherever it is, you definitely don't want to shovel snow. This game is an effective way to get clarity around the details of your dream life - the qualities you're looking for in a partner, the type of place where you'd like to live or work, or even identifying what your most powerful gifts are. You can simply meditate on these questions, or sketch or write out your answers.

Ask the BIG Questions Before You Go to Sleep. Keep a journal by your bed and write down what you dreamed about the night before or take a few minutes to record your thoughts when you first wake up in the morning. Commit to doing this for several days or weeks. Because the answers are already within you, the more you practice tapping into your subconscious the quicker some meaningful patterns will begin to emerge. The answers to everything you're asking are already there. You just have to learn how to listen.

POWER TOOLS

These are powerful methods you can use to start hearing your inner voice more clearly.

RSG Tip: Invest in your dream in the form of a beautiful notebook or journal, or in pictures, stickers or other materials that will make your vision board into something that you're excited to look at.

• **Brainstorm Your Bliss** Another way to find your purpose is to identify the things you like doing – finding those things that make you happy and fulfilled. Brainstorm a list, and write them all down, however insignificant they may seem. If you're not sure, try thinking about the things you enjoyed doing as a child, or something that you've always wanted to do – an idea that just wouldn't go away. Clues to your life purpose, core skills and interests will show up on that list, and even if what you write down seems more like a hobby than a career or life path, be sure to include them. Things that come easily to us are often also those activities that we most enjoy, and our biggest gifts are frequently related to these very things.

When you've got your list then circle the 20 things that you think are most important or that call to you the most. The next day revisit the list and eliminate half of the items you circled until you just have ten left. The next day repeat the exercise until just five items remain. Try to rank these five from most to least important or compelling, then take five to ten minutes to do some stream of consciousness writing on the top two or three topics. Go back and review what you wrote the following day. What is starting to open up for you? What inspired ideas do you have? Write them down.

- **Capture Your Vision** Vision Boards or Vision scrapbooks are excellent tools to start getting clear on your vision and working towards bringing it to life. Try dividing your board or book up into sections such as: home, career, relationships, health, hobbies. Then look for pictures or words that represent some of what you want more of in each of those areas. Again, trust your instincts on this and remove any obstacles or self-imposed limitations. Paste the pictures that you find most compelling on your board or in your book and soon a comprehensive picture of your overall vision will emerge. Whether you end up making a board or a book, keep it somewhere where you can look at it often. The more you're able to integrate those images in your subconscious the quicker they'll start showing up in your life. Again, you don't need to figure out how you're going to achieve anything that's on your vision board or book; you just have to define what it is that you truly want.

- **Volunteer Your Time** If you have tried the above exercises and still have no idea or direction, I strongly recommend finding a way you can volunteer your services. One of the quickest shortcuts to happiness is helping others, and consciously seeking out an opportunity to do this may help to reveal your natural gifts. Don't dismiss this step if you are focused on starting a purpose-driven for-profit business, or if you're considering transforming an existing business to bring it more in alignment with your purpose and calling.

Volunteering by doing something that resonates with you will give you powerful clues as to what your purpose truly is. Your passion for what you're doing, your message and your mission will begin to come into alignment as you use your gifts to help others, and you may be able to use what you're learning from the experience in the professional world. Taking your volunteer experience a step further and building a business around that passion, interest and desire to help others is very often the very thing that leads to great success. People love to follow others who they are inspired by, and those who "walk their walk" fall right into this category.

PAGE OF REFLECTION

Affirmation: *All the answers I seek are within me*

Using adjectives, what are some of the things you want MORE of in your life?

What do you NOT want? What are you currently tolerating?

What common themes do you recognize in your visualization or journaling?

Consider the following:

Friends and Family

Intimate Relationships

Work and Business

Health and Wellness

Travel/ Adventure

Bucket List

What new ideas came from doing these exercises?

CHAPTER 2
The Real Deal

*Authenticity is the daily practice of letting go of who we're
supposed to be and embracing who we are.*
-Brene Brown

Once you get in touch with your inner voice it's time to start sharing that authentic self with the world. Being yourself sounds so simple. Like the easiest thing ever. The reality is, being authentic and speaking from your heart takes courage. Authenticity is closely tied with vulnerability too, because the fact of the matter is, not everyone is going to like what you have to say. If this is something that bothers you, you'd best start getting over that as you prepare to live in alignment with your purpose. You're always going to run into critics, but one thing I've noticed is that most successful people are not overly concerned about what others think of them. They don't spend a lot of time worrying about how they'll be judged for setbacks and failures. And that, my friends, is extremely liberating.

Some people will simply never "get" you. Your message won't resonate with them – they either won't agree with your views, won't understand them or simply will not be interested in what you're doing or what you have to say. As you start to play bigger, some people will judge you before they've even met you. Others will decide they don't like you for seemingly innocuous reasons. But don't worry. Those people are not members of the inner circle that you'll intentionally create. Not everyone is going to be your customer or your ally, but the ones who need to hear your message will find you. The ones who understand – and resonate with – your authentic self will not just actively seek you out; they're going to be your biggest supporters.

Looking back on starting my own business, I realize how naïve I was in so many areas, and one of the biggest of these had to do with this concept of authenticity. When I first declared my video production company open for business more than a decade ago, I thought I could simply target everyone as my customer base. After all, I could get along well with all different kinds of people, and everyone needs great videos, do they not? I thought that as a video production company we could work with pretty much any client, regardless of whether we liked, understood (or even believed in) what they were selling.

Sounds crazy, doesn't it?

Writing those words now makes me cringe a little, because as you probably already know, thinking that everyone can be your customer is a classic rookie move. Trying to be everything to everybody usually means you end up in a wishy-washy mess, and it all comes down to authenticity. This same principle applies to a commercial enterprise as much as it does to your own identity or personal brand.

And this idea is relevant to your life purpose, too. Find your passion and learn to articulate it well and you can ignite and inspire others. When you get people excited about what you're doing or what you're selling they have the potential to become a group of supporters that will propel you forward in unbelievable ways. Energy will build around what you're doing, and you'll be amazed at the synergies that start showing up and the doors that begin to open.

In the world of advertising, these enthusiastic supporters are called "brand advocates" and for a marketer these people are the most valuable and coveted of all demographic groups. Because they understand and relate to you, they gladly share information about what you're doing – often *without even being asked*.

It's difficult – maybe impossible – to buy the loyalty and excitement of a true brand advocate, but these are the people who will be your most valuable allies, and they will find you *because of* – not despite – your authenticity.

Conversely, if you ignore your authentic core and your real purpose, people sense this, and it can be difficult to get them passionately excited about your brand. In my own business we certainly found that to be true. During the time when we were trying to please everyone, we did have customers, but only a smattering of them were actual advocates for our company. Our advocates liked us on a personal level, and they admired our work, but if you asked them what we really stood for or represented none of them could have told you because, quite frankly, we had not done the work to figure this out for ourselves.

When you're looking at identifying a brand for yourself or your business you have to start from the inside out. Now, in my video production company we realized that we stand for teamwork and security. We want customers to know that we've got their back and that we've got their best interests in mind. We treat their business like we treat our own so that they can rest easier at night, knowing they're being well cared for. Some of the best advice I can share with anyone who is starting a business is to stop trying to appeal to the masses and start attracting your tribe to you. Find out what you stand for and deliver that to your customers along with superior service and extra value. Do that and you won't have to go chasing success because it will surely find you.

My sister started her business a few years before I founded my own company, and through a lot of blood, sweat and tears she has built up a successful residential "green" cleaning company. As I was getting started with my own endeavor, I remember her saying, "It's so strange walking down the street and knowing there are people who don't like me. Sometimes I have to stand up to an employee or turn down a client. There are days when you have no choice but to do something that makes you unpopular."

As she shared this story, I distinctly remember thinking, "That's never going to happen to me. Everyone likes me..."

Fast forward a few years and I knew just what she was talking about, having experienced it firsthand on multiple occasions. Of course, some of the people who end up disagreeing with you might be employees (present or past), customers, vendors or any number of trolls on social media. If you're running any type of business or organization, or just trying to manage your own family, some of your decisions won't be popular. Some of them might not even be right, but I believe that when in doubt it's always best to err on the side of being authentic and aligned with your own inner guidance system.

Staying True to You

When you venture out of your comfort zone and do something brave, different, and out of the ordinary, you might hear other voices of protest too. Some people might be jealous of your potential success, especially when they themselves feel stuck or frustrated. Other objections to you following your inner voice might come directly from the people who are closest to you, and they might actually be based in authentic love and concern for you. People will say they won't want you to "get hurt", but not trying to follow your dream risks the biggest hurt of them all: regret for all the chances not taken.

You may not experience anyone else's feedback as you go about fulfilling your purpose, but this is unlikely, so it's best to be prepared. Learn what feedback is likely to sound like, and how to distinguish between positive and negative feedback.

Positive feedback is constructive. The person understands your goals and is simply helping you consider the situation from another perspective. They might say, "Yes, but have you considered doing it this way?" or, "It's great that you want to build your own workshop but I have a friend who can rent you some space so you can get started sooner on chasing your dream."

When you get positive feedback, thank the person and consider what they are suggesting. Maybe you need to sit with the idea for a few days and mull it over with that little voice within yourself. If they're truly aligned with what you're building and do have a way to help you, then perhaps you might want to consider their idea. Or not. You'll know deep down what is right for you. Trust your instinct on this and try to not overthink it too much.

If the feedback you're getting is negative it's going to sound a lot like your negative self-talk. "Oh, but you've never done anything like that before. What makes you think you can do that?" or, "Your father failed with his business. You should just stay with your job because it's safe."

Negative feedback can be hard to move past because it might be very similar to the message you're hearing from your deepest doubts and insecurities (more on that in the next section). This feedback isn't helpful or constructive and will only hold you back. So, if you are subjected to negative feedback, be sure to thank the person for their concern (and really mean it when you say this), and then keep chasing that dream.

The bottom line is, if your voice is calling on you to take inspired action, then that's probably where you should be focusing your attention. At the end of the day the only happiness you are ultimately responsible for is your own and the sooner you can come to terms with the idea that popularity isn't the end goal, the better. By being authentic and allowing your true voice to come out of hiding, you'll begin to attract the right people to you – people who will help you build your business and support you in achieving your goals.

One Courageous Step

Just over a year ago I started a blog series in which I was transparent about some of the struggles my business had faced in the early years. It may not seem like a big deal to publish these stories, but honestly, I found it terrifying. In the blog I was purposely being vulnerable and authentic. I wrote from the heart, but when it came time to publish the articles I hesitated. I was sure my clients would read my posts and dump me, and I was certain that no new clients would want to work with someone who was still figuring out some pretty big issues. But I felt driven to write, and so I did, as openly and honestly as I could muster.

I had made more than my share of missteps in my business and I was determined to turn those events into teaching moments that others could learn from. I made a commitment to myself to be transparent about business and about money, even the less flattering moments. Some of this work culminated in my blog and podcast, and ultimately will be the subject of a future book, but I remember releasing the very first blog article with such a feeling of dread. While we had been blessed with some very, very good times in our business, there were also plenty of dark and scary ones too.

During those less-than-stellar times, money was flowing only one way: out. There were plenty of days when I felt like everything was collapsing around me. On those days I felt like the biggest failure on the planet – drowning under debt and not sure of my next moves. I also felt completely alone, weighed down by the weight of the world on my shoulders.

I had never talked about the tough stuff publicly before, but I was starting to get a sense that my struggles, while somewhat extreme, were certainly not unique. I had a kind of instinct that writing might be the answer, and so my own journey began.

Once I started writing it was hard to stop. I wrote about cash flow struggles, uncertainty, fear and challenges. I wrote about doubts in my own leadership abilities and shared my techniques for working through some of those issues. I wrote about inadequacies, energy and focus. I wrote about unanswerable questions and topics like happiness and freedom. At first, I was posting the articles to a relatively small audience on social media outlets but then I was given an opportunity to publish on larger platforms. The prospect of being more visible was both enticing and daunting, but when I finally said yes to the opportunity something very interesting started to happen.

For one thing, my worst fears never did materialize: I did not lose a single client because of anything I posted. Some of my clients saw the articles and complimented me on them, or even commiserated with me, while others were undoubtedly too busy to even notice. Regardless of whether they responded to what I wrote or not, it truly was business as usual. Apparently being authentic and real did not automatically turn me into a pariah. In fact, the opposite began to happen. I started getting messages and phone calls from business owners all over the country. People expressed gratitude for the articles and told me that my posts were helping them to realize that they were not alone in the types of struggles I was writing about.

Interestingly, I even picked up some new clients because of the blog posts and articles, although that wasn't my intention when writing them. It turns out that the people who were attracted to me because of my authenticity, not in spite of it, ended up becoming some of the most lucrative and fulfilling relationships of my professional career. None of that would have happened, of course, if I hadn't been able to find and embrace that vulnerability or authenticity in the first place.

And although we have navigated those waters and successfully reinvented the business, I keep telling the story of the tough times because other people need to hear that there is hope. Sometimes it may take every ounce of your being to keep going, but the only real failure is when you stop trying.

Emotional Intelligence Sprinkled with Faith

Now, of course, you can be authentic and truthful without being 100% transparent about everything in your business. You need to be emotionally and socially intelligent enough to know when and what to share, and this advice is not intended as a way to justify giving everyone who asks a detailed list of all that ails you. It is a plea to allow yourself to be more open and more vulnerable at the appropriate times. It's a suggestion that you start dabbling in life outside of your comfort zone. Start listening to your intuition and if it's telling you to let your guard down, even just a little, then go ahead and try it. Say yes to doing something that scares you. Voice your opinion. Ask that question. Listen. Being courageous and authentic is something you have to consciously practice, but I promise, it does get easier the more you do it.

And the truth is that sometimes you'll speak from your heart and will find that you don't have a friendly audience. There may be booing and jeers. Trolls and haters may leave comments on your webpages and social media feeds. When that happens it's not pleasant of course, but it's also not the end of the world. For me, the majority of my articles and blog posts received positive feedback. Then, just as I was feeling pretty good about my writing, I received a long scathing comment from a man in Australia. He absolutely hated what I had written. It was about the worst thing he had ever read, or so he said. His comments went on and on and they were far from complimentary. The first time I saw what he had written I was shocked and hurt. How could he say those things about my article? Could I delete his comments before anyone else saw them? What should I do?

I did experience a good 30 seconds of sheer panic but then I remembered a little trick that's saved me more times than I can count: breathe and pause, then repeat. As I took a moment to reflect before reacting to what had happened, I started getting some perspective on the situation. The reality was, my post had gotten the attention of someone as far away as Australia! On some level, that was actually pretty exciting. AND this man had a strong enough reaction to what I had written that he was inspired to reply. Okay, so it wasn't exactly the kind of comment I was hoping to get, but even though he disagreed with me he still felt strongly enough about it to write back. As I considered the situation further, I found that this experience did not make me want to stop writing. Instead, I took it as a sign that writing was exactly what I was supposed to be doing.

As it turns out, the criticism that comes from other people is actually easy to deal with once you detach from needing their approval. It's that other negative voice that poses a much bigger problem.

The Other Voice Within: The Inner Critic

It's not what you say out of your mouth that determines your life; it's what you whisper to yourself that has the most power.
- Robert Kiyosaki

When fear and doubt – your inner critics - enter the picture and wake the sleeping giant within, your dreams could be in serious jeopardy. In fact, that voice is so powerful that it can be difficult or impossible to hear anything else over it. And what types of things are you likely to hear your inner critic saying? Usually it's some reiteration of all the stories that we keep telling ourselves about our own inadequacies, shortcomings and flaws. Your inner critic will gladly list all the reasons that you are unable to do something (fill in the blank with specifics from your own psyche – you know what they are!).

Those stories, and the fear and doubt that goes along with them, have the power to derail even your biggest dreams. Allow me to bequeath upon you a superpower that you can use against your inner critic: the knowledge that the stories he or she tells you are not real. Any supposition about what you can or cannot do, based on some event in your past, exists only in your imagination. Limits that you're placing on yourself because of something that happened in the past, or because of fear of what might happen in the future, exist only in your own mind. Once you grasp this fact and fully embrace it you can begin to proactively shape your reality and create the life you truly desire.

Before we dismiss your inner critic completely, let's take a look at why it exists in the first place.

Your inner critic actually wants to keep you safe, so let's not make it into the bad guy here. Let's just recognize that, as you are looking to move forward, grow, expand and spread your wings, you'll be edging out of familiar territory, and along the way there may be some discomfort. You might stumble, you might make a mistake, someone might not like you, or you may find yourself way outside of your comfort zone.

All of these conditions are signs that you're growing and expanding your horizons and moving closer to your goals. That inner critic sees each of these situations as potential danger and may try to get you to turn back. I encourage you to hear what that little voice is saying, thank him or her for the message, and then keep going. As you begin to get some successes under your belt your inner critic will become less vocal, but that doesn't mean that he or she won't always be there, so you might as well come to peace with that part of yourself.

And what kind of message might that critic be voicing? It usually sounds something like this:

Remember that time you had a party and no one showed up? So how could you possibly think that anyone would come to the workshop that you want to put on?.

The inner critic will let you know that no one in your family has ever made a million dollars, so what gives you the right to think you could do that?

And it's the same voice that says things like, *"You're not smart enough to do that... You're not pretty enough... You're not connected enough."*

Unlike your intuition, this inner voice would serve you better if it were silenced or at least quieted. The easiest way to do that is, ironically, to learn to hear this voice – to become familiar with what it sounds like. Then, when it does show up, you'll be quicker to recognize that it's just doing what it does best: telling stories that have no bearing whatsoever on your future success. The more you keep this voice in check the more likely you are to allow your true and authentic voice to shine, and when that happens you come closer to aligning with your life's purpose.

How to Be Authentic, and Not Care What People Think

*You attract the right things when you have
a sense of who you are.*
-**Amy Poehler**

This chapter has been all about the concept of honoring the person that you truly are, not just who people expect you to be. Sometimes being true to yourself might be difficult or uncomfortable. You also have to recognize and celebrate the fact that not everyone is going to share your thoughts and opinions. Our differences are what make the world so special and magical, and when you're showing up as yourself and for yourself you are contributing to the incredible fabric that is our humanity.

Being authentic is about being yourself, bettering yourself and furthering your dreams and potential. It is not about controlling or harming others. This is your path and yours alone. Others may choose to walk parts of it with you, but other times you may feel like you're venturing into unknown territory alone. Hold onto your vision and trust that the process will work for you, because it always does.

And please keep in mind that you can be both authentic and kind to others whose opinions don't align with yours. Some people think that in order to be authentic you have to be completely raw and unfiltered all the time, but there are ways to be assertive and authentic and to still do so with grace and kindness. When in doubt, err on the side of being kind – both to yourself and to others.

Here are some exercises to help you get in touch with and honor your authentic self.

POWER TOOLS

- Practice speaking up for yourself in little ways until you get used to doing it – assertiveness, like anything, takes practice. Being assertive is never an excuse to be unkind or demeaning, but the next time you're out to eat and your order is wrong, or you want dressing on the side, say something - but do it respectfully. The more you do this the easier it gets, and you'll be better prepared to speak up when it really matters.

- Check in with yourself: are your words and actions in line with your purpose/inner voice? Are you walking your talk?

- Consider these questions: what are your intentions? Are you trying to truly help someone or are you motivated solely by self-gain?

- Are you being open-minded? You are not required to take the criticisms, doubts, fears and negativity of anyone else on as your own baggage, but sometimes it can be helpful to hear another point of view. Can you set respectful boundaries that allow you to listen without defending yourself or arguing with the other person?

- Are you speaking, acting and listening from your heart?

- Are you trying to force or convince someone else to do something? By all means, share your point of view if the other person is open to hearing it. If the person is not ready to receive your information, or if your point of view is out of line with their values and ideas, don't push it. You are not responsible for anyone else's happiness or life choices.

- It's okay if not everyone agrees with you. Our differences are what make us interesting. The more you continue to speak with an authentic voice the more likely you are to attract a tribe of people who "get" and value you.

- Are you looking for validation, happiness or worth somewhere outside of yourself? If so, stop and regroup. Happiness is a personal choice and it's fully unconditional on what anyone else does, says or has.

PAGE OF REFLECTION

Affirmation: *I honor and respect my inner being*

Values exercise

Brainstorm all the values that you think are important for YOU. Your list can be as long as you'd like.

Now, go back to the list and pick out the top four values that mean the most to you. Why are these so important? How do you honor them on a regular basis?

Intentionally designing your dream life means getting in touch with what's important to you. What are you going to be sure to include in your life plan based on these exercises? Did these exercises help you to see something that was missing that you might not have recognized before?

What new ideas came up during these exercises?

CHAPTER 3
The Path

You never know where life is going to take you. So, everything I do, I just take it one day at a time, and it always leads you to the right place.
-**Kyle Massey**

We've all had experiences in our lives where we could say with certainty that we were in the right place at the right time. There was that time we literally bumped into the cute guy or gal in a crowded restaurant and ended up in a long-term relationship. Or the day we found ourselves in a job interview with the exact person with whom we had just exchanged pleasantries in the coffee shop. Or the time you picked up the phone and cold called a potential client who said yes, which was the beginning of a lucrative long-term partnership. Everyone has these stories, but what if I told you that you're always (yes, always) in the right place at the right time and that life is always (yes, always) working out in your favor?

I'm going to go out on a limb and say that many of you would probably call me bat-shit crazy. You'd start listing off all the times that you lost the client, weren't able to pay the bills, missed out on getting the house you were trying to buy... You might tell me that you're just not lucky, that all the good stuff just seems to pass you by. And yet, no matter how hard you tried to convince me of all the missed opportunities I would still say that no, you really are always in the right place.

How can that be?

Essentially, at any given time you're experiencing one of two things. You're either succeeding wildly at life, you're finding out what you don't want, or you're learning valuable lessons that will serve you well one day and will help propel you further along your path.

But what is my path in life supposed to look like?

Well, your path would be extremely easy to navigate if it were possible for you to see into your future or if you could study the giant road map that shows you just how everything in your life is supposed to fit together. But wouldn't that take the fun and adventure out of it? And anyway, it's a rhetorical statement because we're simply not privy to that information. We only get to see the big picture after the fact, when we're looking back on how everything played out and how every experience drove us closer to our purpose. And then it all makes perfect sense. Even the so-called bad stuff. Even the struggles, the pain and the moments that seemed unbearable. It's the ultimate "ah-ha" moment, but one we don't get to experience until much later. In the meantime, we have to learn how to play the system.

The good news is, in this game the odds are stacked in your favor. There is also an important shortcut that you need to know about. The quickest way to get to a place of success and alignment with your purpose is to understand and accept that you're always being nudged back into a place that's serving your higher self. Once you understand this and accept it as fact, you'll be more open to tuning into the breadcrumbs that the Universe is leaving for you to follow. When you're able to recognize these clues and act on them with faith and intuition, you'll be on the fast track to success.

So, how do you start to receive those messages? Well, some people adopt an analytical process and make a list of their goals and values. They then evaluate each new decision they are faced with based on whether a particular action gets them nearer or farther from their target. Others take a more alternative approach – looking for affirmative signs in synchronicities, numerology or even in finding objects such as coins or feathers.

Learning to Follow the Flow

Personally, I think that if one of these methods resonates with you and if you get value from it then, by all means, listen to the messages you are receiving. However, in this chapter I'd like to talk more in depth about "flow" and how you can tap into that state of being by tuning into your intuition and by being open to receiving the signs that the Universe is sending your way.

So, what does that guidance look like? Well, sometimes it's subtle and other times it is very dramatic, fast and furious. If you're veering off your life path or purpose, then I can promise you that the Universe is going to let you know about it, softly at first, then increasingly loudly until you simply have to pay attention.

Oprah has a saying about learning to listen as your life whispers to you, because, as she says, if you ignore those whispers you end up getting nudged, prodded and pushed, and if you still don't listen then eventually you'll be "hit on the head with a brick". It won't be a physical brick, of course – most of the time, anyway – but the type of thing that does frequently happen when people are on the wrong path is that they end up getting sick, injured, fired, or some other seemingly negative consequence that forces that person to make some dramatic shifts in how they're doing things.

When you are in the "flow", the feedback that you receive will be more positive and encouraging. In this state things are easy. When you're in that place of receiving, although you may be hustling, nothing feels difficult or like much of a chore. You're riding the wave and having fun. Almost as if by magic you're being introduced to the right people at opportune times and you may find that money starts coming your way in new and unexpected ways. You are excited about life and are happy to both give and receive the gifts of the Universe. You feel good, you look good and your energy is magnetic. When you're in this state you are most likely experiencing life in alignment with your purpose even though you may not be able to articulate exactly what your purpose is at this point.

Things are Always Working Out for You

The first time I remember experiencing what it was like to be in the flow in a "big way" was after graduating from college. In my final semester I had taken an internship in a field I thought I wanted to pursue, but I quickly discovered in no uncertain terms that that was not the career path for me.

After a brief identity crisis, I realized that, while pivoting at that stage in life may be a blow to my ego, it wasn't actually all that difficult. With no responsibilities beyond the obligatory student loan payments, the whole world seemed full of opportunities, leaving me open to choose the path I wanted to follow. I did a bit of research and decided that, with my intended career path temporarily derailed, I would move to the Czech Republic. At that time I was told it was relatively easy to get a job teaching English in any of the former Soviet Bloc countries and I was up for a little adventure. I wasn't sure what to expect, but I think that I had a vision of stepping off the plane and getting swooped up by a rich and glamorous company. That, however, is not exactly the way things turned out.

Before leaving the States, I had compiled a list of language schools that were advertising for native English speakers. This was before the Internet was widespread, so my resources consisted of printouts of addresses and phone numbers of a variety of language schools and some handwritten notes. One by one I visited the schools and was told time and time again that none of the current openings were appropriate for me. As this trend continued throughout my first week in the country, and then the second, I was starting to get a little scared and nervous. I had knocked on a great many doors and was beginning to realize that I had gone into this little adventure without a very good back-up plan. Luckily, that was right about the time that the flow of the Universe started to kick in.

In the end, I didn't end up with the glamorous job I may have been expecting, but the way things unfolded was most definitely aligned with my life's purpose. In fact, the job I did get would eventually lead to amazing things, including meeting my future husband, living in a prime location in Prague, working in exciting and challenging jobs in radio and film production and years of travel and adventure. Twenty years after I first arrived in Prague, I founded my own video production company in New York directly because of experience and contacts I had gained all those years before.

And how did I get that first job? I want to share this story with you because I think it illustrates quite well what the flow of the Universe often looks like. When none of my planned job search tactics were working out I decided to take the day off and meet a friend for a drink in a smoky café. It was on my way to the restroom that I stopped to peruse the bulletin board. There, hidden underneath all the flyers, ads and notices was an index card with a handwritten job description. The card said that an English teacher was needed in a place I'd never heard of called Domazlice. I had no idea where that town was, or anything about it, but I felt drawn to the ad and, later that day, went off to the post office to place the call.

The headmaster of the high school answered, and as it turned out the ad had been tacked up on that board for months and they had actually hired a teacher several weeks before I set foot in the café. But (and here's where it gets interesting) not long before I rang, the teacher who was lined up to take the position had called to decline, citing personal issues. The school year was about to start, and the headmaster was worried about not being able to cover all of the English classes. As it turned out, my timing was perfect. Needless to say, I did get the job and that one decision directly or indirectly led to every significant thing that has happened in my life since. It's incredible to think about it now, but the fact that the timing was so perfect was a giant clue that the opportunity was the right one for me to say yes to. My actions at the time were solely driven by instinct. I never could have orchestrated or planned that course of events, but in hindsight it's easy to see how significant – and how perfect - it really was.

When that kind of thing happens, the Universe is telling you:

> *"Yes, you are on the exact right path at the exact right time."*
> -**Elin Barton**

That story was an example of what "flow" looks like, where things are easily – and obviously - working out for you. Flow is exactly what it sounds like. It's the opposite of struggle. Flow is going along with things, being tuned into what your instincts are guiding you to do. It's trusting that the Universe really does have you covered, and that it's always putting the right people and situations in your path at just the right time.

Not only do all of us have the ability to operate and navigate through life in that state, but I've come to believe that it's actually our most natural and highest state of being. Problems only come up when we start to overthink things and question our decisions. That's when it gets a lot less fun and when we typically start getting in our own way.

Digging Deeper

Let's deconstruct the steps required to get to "flow" and look at them one by one, as they relate to the story I just shared. I started the events in motion by taking the initiative to go over to the Czech Republic in the first place. That decision was made partly by logic, partly by instinct, and largely by something I call "following your bliss".

I took that first step, flew over the ocean, then, once I got there, I moved into action, knocking on a great many doors. When none of them opened I just kept knocking (staying "in action"). I only ended up finding my perfect position when I stepped away from my original plan of working for one of the schools on my list. The magic was only able to kick in when I took the all-important step of "releasing", and allowing the right thing to come to me.

While that example illustrates how things look when you are on the right path, clues that you're on the wrong path are equally important to recognize, and they often feel like you're hitting one roadblock after another. Sometimes we continue along a blocked and difficult path because that's all we know. Without the knowledge that there is an easier and quicker way to reach our goals, many of us continue beating our way through a jungle that is overgrown with challenges and obstacles. We work too hard, stress too much and stray far away from our real purpose and bliss.

Of course, as the creator of your own reality and orchestrator of your own life you are free to make those decisions. If you commit to seeking out "flow" in your life it means that you're always looking for the blessings and the opportunities. You begin to believe that people come into your world on purpose, either to learn from you or to teach you something. You stop getting upset when things don't go just as you have thought they would because you recognize that everything is happening for your greater good, even when it's not immediately obvious. When you step into a place of faith you open the doors of your life to true miracles and you also release a lot of stress and worry.

> *I am in the right place, at the right time,*
> *doing the right thing.*
> -**Louise L. Hay**

Have you ever been disappointed or upset when one of these seemingly negative experiences showed up in your life? Maybe you were fired from a job or had to move out of a house or apartment before you were ready to. Maybe a relationship ended, you lost someone close to you or a business deal didn't work out the way you intended.

At the time when we are experiencing any one of these circumstances it's easy to get caught up in hurt, disappointment, loss, grief, fear or shame. The way life unfolds, painful events frequently open up possibilities for something new and better to show up for you. At a minimum, living through a painful circumstance will change you in some way and may allow you to help someone who is dealing with a similar challenge down the road. Other losses frequently bring with them opportunities that never would have been there before. That's why learning to flip the tables and view disappointments as opportunities is another way to quickly bring you in close alignment with your soul's purpose.

The next time one of these difficult situations appears for you, try welcoming it instead of resisting by asking the question, "What are you here to teach me?"

Then be open to hearing the answers.

Learn to Listen to Your Inspired Thoughts

You might receive an inspired thought during meditation or in dreams. Or the answers may come to you when you're journaling or doing other reflective work. You might start hearing clues in things other people are saying to you. Or someone might give you a book or recommend a movie that has an important message for you. The clues are going to show up regardless of whether you're tuned into seeing them, so why not start paying closer attention?

Mary struggled for years with her business. She tried idea after idea, to no avail. Mary networked and put herself out there, she created online courses and digital offerings, yet nothing was giving her any significant traction, or the growth she was looking for in her business. Then one day a few years ago she started talking about wanting to start a mastermind group. The idea of this group kept coming up for her. It was the nagging idea that wouldn't go away, until it turned into a burning desire.

Mary started telling people she wanted to join such a group and before long she started hearing about opportunities to do just that. Over the next couple of years, she tried out different groups and took note of the dynamics of each of them. Some groups were run well but others had some major flaws. Mary paid attention to all of it, and over time she began to see herself as someone who could lead these groups.

Although Mary's core business never took off the way she intended, she did acquire a high level of business knowledge and experience. It may not have served her in the way she originally wanted it to, but as a group facilitator she is helping hundreds of people to grow their businesses while also making a comfortable living. As it turns out, the perfect role for Mary was not the one she set out to create for herself.

What Mary did right was to work hard at her business. She tried many different avenues to make that original business work and was open to learning new skills along the way. At the same time, she followed her interests and talked to people about what she was looking for. Opportunities began to appear, and when they showed up she took them, setting her on course to create a dream job that was truly aligned with her purpose.

Mary's path to success may not have been predictable, neat or tidy, but does it matter that it took her a little time to figure out what her purpose is? Was all her time spent running a struggling business wasted? Do people consider her a failure for the challenges that she faced? No, of course not. It was precisely because of her experience and struggles that she became such a good coach.

I'm sure that when she was struggling and frustrated in business Mary did not see herself as a successful business coach. That was the last thing that she felt she could become, in fact. But the biggest thing she did right was to keep trying different avenues and knocking on a lot of doors. Then, as she started developing the desire to pursue the mastermind groups she took the time not only to listen but also to take the actions required to make that happen.

Having faith through the tough times will make you happier. But true success only comes when you master the ability to keep moving forward.
-Elin Barton

In this chapter we are talking a lot about your purpose and some may interpret that as meaning that each of us has a predetermined fate, but that is not the way that I see it. Certainly, there are gifts we're each given and other lives we are supposed to touch, but there is one important component that must be mentioned, and that is free will. We all have free will, which means that we can choose to act in alignment with our higher self – or not – at any point along our path.

The more we resist, the longer it may take us to find our purpose, but, like swimming in a river with a current, I believe we're always going in the direction of our higher selves and purpose.

That means if you should miss one sign or opportunity along the way, there will be another and another. The trick is to learn to see those opportunities and then to take action on the ones we find most intriguing.

Remember that life is a giant adventure and there are plenty of paths you can take on your way to purpose, fulfillment and happiness. Let go of needing to know how you're going to get there and get focused on enjoying the ride along the way.

Trying to control the "how" and forcing yourself on a particular path that may not be aligned with your higher self can set you up for a life of struggle. Instead of being open to seeing opportunities you walk around with blinders on, seeing only one possible path to success, when in reality there are an infinite number of options.

This limited thinking not only puts way too much pressure on people. It also causes them to give away the power around creating their own success and happiness. If you see only one possible path to success then it becomes incredibly important to land that particular client, get that particular job or date that specific person.

The truth is, going through life with this attitude limits your possibilities. It's kind of like going to a buffet that's been laid out by gourmet chefs and deciding in advance that you're only going to have bread and butter. I mean, it's good to have a plan but make sure there's enough flexibility in that plan to stay open to the delights that life has in store for you.

Taking the Scenic Route

Remember, detours and diversions along your journey are not signs of failure. On the contrary, they make the journey more interesting and you will still end up in the same general place in the end as long as you keep going. The key to all of this is to keep up momentum, exploring possibilities, asking the questions and knowing that things are always ultimately working out for your higher good.

Relax. You don't have to figure out every little thing in advance. In fact, you could never predict half the things that life is going to surprise you with, so sit back and enjoy the ride.
-Elin Barton

When you start hitting challenges, disappointments and other roadblocks you might find yourself getting scared or retreating into survival mode. When you're feeling fear, lack and scarcity it can seem as if nothing at all is going your way. You may start to lose your confidence with life. Instead of dancing a sexy tango with faith and flow you might feel like you're out of step with the world. That can be a very scary place and it is when many people will start to desperately try to control every aspect of their lives. They might withdraw inwardly and stop believing in their own magnificence.

When things aren't going well you might start to hear some of your old stories coming up: how you're not good enough, not smart enough, not whatever enough. Although we all experience self-doubt from time to time, this is an unhealthy and unproductive place to pitch your tent long-term. While I don't want to spend too much time dwelling on what it's like when things are tough, I do want to paint a good enough picture so the next time this happens for you, you can quickly recognize the situation and hit the "pause" button.

When things aren't going well, give yourself a break. Pause. Breathe. Regroup. And then give thanks for all that you're being taught.
-Elin Barton

A Matter of Perspective

Sometimes it's hard for us to pull back and see the bigger picture when we're in the midst of worry or struggle, so training yourself to rewire your brain around all of this is critical. Consciously and intentionally stay open to finding the lessons and opportunities in whatever you're experiencing. Also remember that in life everything ebbs and flows. Your current crisis might look very different a few months or years down the road, so try to mentally put yourself there in the future, in a place where the problem has been solved and you've achieved a successful outcome.

n the midst of a crisis, if you find yourself caught up in what could/ should/ would have been, then I think it's only fair that you also take a look at what has worked in your life. Every one of us has times when we've gotten "lucky" by being blessed by so-called coincidences, synchronicities or even miracles, many of which have emerged out of challenging situations.

We've all been on the path of flow at one time or another. We've had the right person show up in our lives at just the right time. We've gotten a job, had an opportunity or experienced some other blessing because we listened to what we were being called to do; we stepped up and took some kind of action. It's important to acknowledge and remember your own successes. You've overcome adversity so many times in the past that surely you can do it again. And doesn't it get easier and easier each time? That's what life's about. Yes, sometimes there is pain and the lessons are tough, but all of us are just prepping us for what is to come.

The miracles are always there so why not start expecting them to show up? Going through life welcoming these miracles is one of the most powerful gifts we can give ourselves, because what life has in store for us is far greater than what we could have dreamed up on our own. And sometimes those miracles are disguised as failures or setbacks, so be open to seemingly "bad" things having a silver lining.

If you take in all of this information – about being in the flow and the idea that everything that happens to you is for your eventual well-being - then you'll begin to understand that there is no wrong place, and there is no wrong time. When you are able to understand and accept this, life becomes more fun. You experience real freedom as you don't have to be so worried about getting everything perfect because you realize that it already is exactly as it should be. You get to relax more, and when you're finally less fearful about avoiding all bad experiences (remember, the contrast of good and bad, joy and pain, gifts and loss are all a part of everyone's human experience), you'll be freer and braver about taking chances and about achieving your real dreams and desires.

POWER TOOLS:

Practice being in a "flow" state by calming your mind. You can't be open to the magic of the Universe if you're consumed by worry and chatter in your mind.

A good way to do this is to get in the habit of sitting quietly at the same time every day, or several times throughout the day. Aim for 5-15 minutes; whatever is comfortable for you. You can concentrate on the action of your breathing, and when you notice thoughts infiltrating into your mind, you can acknowledge them and then let them go. You can also use a meditation app. There are several good free ones that are available.

When you've managed to quiet your mind, remind yourself that the Universe always has your back. Make this your mantra.

Then start looking for what inspires you and what feels right. Begin to trust your instincts and to act on them. If you are sitting at your desk and suddenly your aunt Mary's face comes to mind, pick up the phone and call her. Tell her what you're up to. Let it go, without any expectations of HOW that conversation might lead to something that will eventually help you on your journey. Remember, you don't have to understand HOW it's all going to happen, you just have to learn to listen, act, and trust the process.

PAGE OF REFLECTION

Affirmation: *I am always in the right place at the right time*.

Every challenge brings opportunities and lessons.

A Blessing in Disguise

Describe a time when you didn't get a job or other opportunity
– something that was disappointing, but which actually left you
open to receiving something even better. What can you learn
from this?

Navigating a challenge – especially when you're feeling stuck

Sit in a quiet place, close your eyes and imagine yourself in the
future. You have successfully navigated this challenge and you
are once again living your best life. Observe the scene around
you in detail.

Now open your eyes and write down a list of all the possible
ways you could have solved your problem. Nothing is too crazy
to include on this list! Write everything down that you can think of.

Now, go back through the list and see if you can identify one
or two actionable steps that you can take right now to move
forward toward a successful outcome.

What new ideas came up during these exercises?

CHAPTER 4
The "F" Words

*"The greatest glory in life lies not in never falling
but in rising up every time we fall."*
– Nelson Mandela

Failure and Fear.

There you have it. Two big "F" words that go hand in hand.

Let's face it: neither of these is something that's much fun to contemplate. In fact, both fear and failure make people downright uncomfortable. These aren't topics for light dinner conversations. Most of us don't want to dwell on either fear or failure, because doing that is the opposite of our favorite "F" word: fun.

And isn't that the truth? Winning is fun. Who doesn't want to cheer the winning team, bask in the glow of success, or pat themselves on the back for making clever picks in the stock market?

But failure? Not so much. People talk about shame, guilt or loss when they describe their failures. Words like sadness or depression frequently come up, as do feelings of unworthiness and inadequacy.

Because not many of us consciously choose to seek out experiences of loss, guilt, shame and sorrow, we often simply avoid those situations that put us at risk of failure. In fact, research done on this topic indicates that avoidance or procrastination are two common reactions to situations where failure is perceived as a likely or even as a possible outcome.

Interestingly, at the same time that fear of failure can be paralyzing, most of us will overestimate the likelihood that something will go wrong if we try something new, and so we're less inclined to take the risk. It's simply easier and more comfortable to stick with the status quo and to keep doing things the way we've always done them.

The thing is, this tendency to stay safe – or at least to work to avoid public humiliation or failure – is also what keeps us playing small. We avoid risk, but that means that we also could miss opportunities for big wins and spectacular success.

The fact of the matter is, most things worth doing almost always involve some level of risk. And if you're going to truly step forth into an entrepreneurial venture or make the decision to "walk your talk" and live in a way that is in line with your purpose, there is a chance that things might not go exactly as you have planned. And here's the mic drop moment: failure is neither absolute nor final. It's something we should celebrate.

Just Keep Swimming

As long as we learn from our so-called failures then they truly are bringing us one step closer to success. The trick of it is simply to let go of judgment about how good or bad you're doing, and to just keep moving forward. In my experience, we all have days when we feel like everything is an utter mess of black and gooey ugliness. Everywhere we turn it seems like things are going wrong, but that's a short-term view. The reality is, as long as you maintain some kind of momentum and focus on your end game, you will eventually land on the right path. The only way you're not going to end up where you want to be is if you allow yourself to become stagnant and bogged down. If you need to pause and regroup, then go ahead and do that, but then get up and keep going. You may not know exactly what action you should be taking and it's not all that important... just keep knocking on lots and lots of doors and see what opportunities begin to reveal themselves.

Sometimes, as author Mike Dooley says, it's a matter of picking the "least sucky option," and that's okay. The only thing that is *not* an option is taking no action at all.

There are hundreds of examples of famously successful people who first endured a great many failures. J.K. Rowling was a struggling single mother and was living in true poverty when she wrote the first Harry Potter book. She famously received "loads" of rejections of that manuscript before it was picked up by Bloomsbury and she ultimately became one of the world's wealthiest women and most successful and widely read authors.

Abe Lincoln is one of the most important American presidents, yet he famously failed at multiple businesses and unsuccessfully ran for office six times before being elected president. During the course of his struggles his beloved fiancée died, and he had a nervous breakdown, yet he persisted.

Steve Jobs was fired from his own company in a devastating blow, but he later said at a commencement speech he gave at Stanford, "I didn't see it then, but it turned out that getting fired from Apple was the best thing that could have ever happened to me. The heaviness of being successful was replaced by the lightness of being a beginner again, less sure about everything. It freed me to enter one of the most creative periods of my life."

The list goes on and on, but the thing that all the famous failures and eventual successes have in common is that those so-called failures turned out to be nothing more than temporary roadblocks, challenges, and bumps in the road. While I'm certain the "failures" were extremely painful and difficult at the time, in all cases they helped pave a new and better road forward.

It's All Fun and Games in the Rear-View Mirror

When you're in a place where you feel like things aren't going your way there can be a tendency to think that you're the only one who is struggling. We all like receiving the accolades, successes, shiny trophies and gold stars. The Internet doesn't help. Most social media feeds are a compilation of carefully curated posts that make it appear that everyone is having a life that's more fun, glamorous and successful than yours is. They can make it seem so easy and seamless that you might start to feel pretty bad about your own struggles.

The part that we're usually not privy to is all the hard work and inevitably, the thousand times that wildly successful person stumbled, fell, got back up and did it all again. You don't see the sleepless nights, when fear and doubt stealthily creep in, and you also don't see conversations with well-meaning friends and family members who said, "Are you sure about this? Wouldn't it be safer to get a job/stay where you are/ go back to school...?

You also don't see the sliver of fear that, at one time or another, the now-successful CEO, actor, artist or writer certainly experienced, back when they were standing right where you are now, wondering how or if things were going to work out for them.

Learn from the Failure – Don't Wallow in It

Anyone who has achieved success has also overcome significant adversity. In my work with fellow entrepreneurs I have found that, without exception, we've all faced significant challenges along the way.

Some of us have temporarily put our dreams on hold and have gotten a job, offered a product or service that we weren't overly excited about, reinvented and reimagined ways to keep moving forward. Whatever temporary solution we happened to come up with might have felt dismal or inadequate at the time, but again, it's all about persevering and moving forward.

> *"I never fail. I either succeed or I learn."*
> -**Unknown**

What is indisputable is that on life's path sometimes things simply will not go the way you want them to. You may lose money, clients, accounts, friends or relationships, but none of these things are worth beating yourself up over. It may not immediately be apparent, but I'd be willing to bet that your perceived failure is actually setting you up for something better down the road.

And when this happens to you (and it will), keep in mind that YOU are not the failure. The challenge you're facing – however daunting it may seem - is simply something that you're experiencing in that particular space or time. It cannot define you unless you allow it to, which means you have the power to make a completely different choice. Remember, the world is ever-changing and so if you're having a hard time, remember, it's not going to last forever. Incidentally, the same principles apply when you're experiencing big successes. Acknowledge, celebrate and enjoy the good times and when the waters get rough again remember that you will get back to a better place as long as you keep moving forward.

An Opportunity to Learn and Grow

Take away the judgment and successes and failures simply become experiences. Either way you're getting feedback that something is working or it's not. You're either on course or you have to make a correction in your navigation.

Experiencing failure doesn't mean you're doomed forever. It's feedback and it's temporary. In fact, you could even look at it as a gift of sorts. When you fail at something the Universe is simply nudging you closer to your true purpose, to the path you're supposed to be on.

Okay, so at the time it might not feel like a gentle and loving nudge. I get that.

But you have to admit that if you're being honest, you can look back on a challenge that you faced earlier in life and see the value in the experience. Every failure brings with it some kind of lesson, and if you don't learn the lesson, life has a funny way of teaching it to you again and again.

The next time you're faced with what some might call a failure, hit the "pause" button. Instead of getting upset or immediately criticizing and over-analyzing yourself, try getting curious around the situation. Instead of having the same old conversation with yourself, try reframing it in a, "Hello, Failure. What are you here to teach me? I'm listening..." kind of way.

Failure as a Stepping Stone to Success

The more you learn to welcome failure as a stepping stone to success, the less fear will even show up for you. Learn to embrace the possibility of failure, to lean into it, and you'll be far ahead of the crowd. Most people who find success do so by making friends with failure. Sarah Blakely, the founder of Spanx, and one of the wealthiest female entrepreneurs in the world, tells a story about how her father would encourage his children to try to fail every day and then to share stories of those failures at the dinner table. If the kids didn't have a story to share, he'd be disappointed, and they'd have to try again the next day. Sarah said that the more she and her siblings learned to talk about their failures in a matter-of-fact way, the more willing they became to take risks. Getting over the fear of failure – and rejection – is what Sarah Blakely claims is one of the great secrets to her incredible success.

> *"Success is not final; fear is not fatal;*
> *it is the courage to continue that counts."*
> –**Winston Churchill**

In my own experience, it was only in surrendering to failure that I started learning what I was truly capable of. Failing actually catapulted me onto a path that was in line with my purpose, but going through it was no walk in the park.

I knew that my business had been facing some challenges, but I was under the impression that I had everything under control. In fact, I was trying to control everything SO much that the Universe may have been trying to help me, but I couldn't see it. Then one day my world turned upside down.

Our big problem was cash flow. We had lost a big client and in a desperate bid for survival we started chasing any opportunity for work that could bring in money and help pay the bills. We began selling our services for less than they were worth and that very quickly became an unsustainable model.

If you had asked me what my purpose was during that time, I would have struggled to answer the question. I would have been able to talk about the numbers we were trying to reach, our financial goals and how far we were from reaching them. I would have been able to tell you the earning potential from any number of clients that we were pursuing. Beyond all of that, I would have been hard-pressed to articulate our mission.

Looking back, it's clear why it was so tough to sign any contracts. The clients might not have known the details, but their "Spidey Senses" were tingling. On some visceral level I'm sure they could sense that I was being driven mainly by fear, rather than by passion and excitement for them and their projects.

It was a proverbial train wreck waiting to happen and when it did, it wasn't pretty. As the business imploded my worst nightmares came to life. I experienced failure, shame and every possible twist and turn on the roller coaster of negative emotions.

It was horrifying and paralyzing. But during those dark days I realized something. Everything that I had worked so hard to avoid had happened. I wasn't able to stop the tidal wave, but when it happened, I was given a gift, and that gift was to stop expending my energy fighting off the inevitable. I didn't realize how much effort I had been putting into holding everything together.

Letting go of it all wasn't my decision - it happened because eventually I was no longer able to stave it off. The days that followed the implosion were rough, but then I realized something: even though the worst, most horrible thing had happened, I had survived it. Yes, I was knocked down and it was most definitely messy, but one of the advantages of starting from zero is that you have nothing to lose.

My family was counting on me to figure things out, so I did. I started over with all the steps we've talked about in this book - envisioning the outcome, knocking on many doors, and with a deep faith that things really were working out for me (despite all evidence to the contrary!).

I became deeply tapped into gratitude and I started talking to people about the kind of company I wanted to build. It took a little time but eventually gained momentum. Now I have a different company. It's stronger, leaner and more agile than before. We understand our work and our purpose, and as soon as we were able to declare that we started seeing more and more of the right clients showing up.

No longer afraid

To be honest, I never would have opted into experiencing the ordeal that I described above. It was pretty bad and absolutely no fun! Now that I'm out on the other side, I have the battle scars, but I have something else too: a deep knowledge that I do not need to be afraid.

The worst has already happened, and I figured it out.

That's incredibly liberating.

If necessary, I'll do it again, and in the meantime so many people have told me that this story has helped them with their own struggles and that it feels like it was all part of some crazy divine plan. Now, the challenges are fewer and farther between. When they do show up, they are much easier to ride out. This is both because I have more knowledge and more tools at my disposal, and it's also because I no longer waste time and energy trying to keep failure at bay. Channeling the energy to more constructive causes has made all the difference.

PAGE OF REFLECTION

Affirmation: *I choose to embrace and learn from failure.*

What are you afraid of?

Sit quietly for a few minutes and let your mind go to the thing you are most afraid of. If it's financial ruin, losing your house, your friends and family scorning you, or any number of other things, just look at it in your mind's eye.

Sit with it, however unpleasant this may be. See yourself in this place, and once you can clearly see it, envision yourself moving through and beyond the place of failure. You're rebuilding again. Your true friends are there supporting you – or maybe you've got new and better friends by your side.

Allow yourself to see a new and better reality; one in which you've faced your worst fears and come out the other side.

What would you do if you knew that you could not fail?

This question has been posed on greeting cards and magnets everywhere, but that's because it's a good one. If failure was not an option what lofty goals would you pursue? What dreams would come true for you? Write it all down, then consider the possibility that maybe these things ARE possible for you, especially when you do not have to figure out the HOW part of the equation.

What new ideas came up during these exercises?

PART 2
Set

Learning to come to terms with time and money, and intentionally building your tribe lays the groundwork for your greatest successes.

And of course, since your thoughts shape your reality, you have to learn how to expect that which you most want to receive...

CHAPTER 5
Time Shifter

"I mark the hours, every one,
Nor have I yet outrun the sun.
My use and value, unto you,
Are gauged by what you have to do"
- Inscription inside Hermione Granger's
borrowed Time-Turner

"Three turns should do it."
- J.K. Rowling, *Harry Potter and*
the *Prisoner of Azkaban*

I nearly spit my coffee out all over the table when my friend Tara told me what she thought of the way my life had been going so far.

> *"You're just like Swiss cheese," she said, nibbling on her biscotti.*

> *I looked at her incredulously. "What? I don't understand."*

> *"You go through life like you're going down one of the holes, then you hit a roadblock and you just go through another hole. It's exactly like moving through a block of cheese, but it's actually kind of a beautiful thing."*

That conversation stuck with me, perhaps partly because I had never been compared to a block of cheese before, but also because what Tara said really resonated with me. The first time or two you find that you have to pivot it might feel a little scary, but it does get easier.

Ironically, change is one of the few constants in life. We think we're going in a certain direction, and that might work out for a while but then (darn it!) we change, evolve and find that we're no longer aligned with the path we thought was so right for us.

Or your customers change. Or it's the market. Or technology.

Whatever the case may be, the sooner you come to peace with the fact that you're not going to be able to predict everything, the better. Take Covid, for example. Nobody really saw that one coming and suddenly the whole world had to adapt and change. Yes, that presented us with enormous challenges, but it also provided many individuals and businesses with new opportunities to grow and reinvent themselves.

There is always opportunity in any crisis, whether it's a challenge in your business, the economy or a global pandemic. The people who keep their head and don't panic and who can look just a little bit into the future are the ones who are going to not only survive, but who will thrive when things get tough.

When we run into blocks or challenges in business and in life many of us instinctually pull back and resist what we perceive as a negative situation. Imagine the opportunities that could be open to you if you did the opposite. What if instead, you embraced change? What if the opportunity to pivot was something that was to be coveted, not shied away from?

It's an interesting concept, especially when you consider that if you currently don't have everything you want in your life, then you're going to have to start doing some things differently. You know that old saying about a sign of insanity being someone who keeps doing the same thing over and over again but expecting different results?

Many people try to resist change or to find some fault with it, but the truth is, change is the only thing you can ever really count on.

How does that statement make you feel? Excited? Fearful? Anxious?

Many people are deeply afraid of change and stay stuck, clinging to old beliefs, ideas, jobs and relationships that no longer serve them. But because change is the natural way of the Universe, and because it's (ironically) the one constant we can count on, hanging onto the old stuff not only stops you from getting what you really want, it also takes an inordinate amount of energy that could be better spent building something new.

Let's put esoteric discussions aside for the moment and focus instead on something that is very familiar to you, to demonstrate this idea of constant change. You've been living with your own body for a long time now, so let's start there. Most people would tell you that they're inhabiting the same body they started out this life with, but is this really true?

By the time you're reading this book the body that you call your own probably bears very little resemblance to the baby version of yourself who was brought into the world a good number of years ago. Sure, you may be able to see glimpses of your present self when you study your baby pictures, or your future self when you look in the mirror now, but all the biological matter that makes you unique – all of the cells that comprise your body – those are not the same cells that you started out with. Many of these cells aren't even the same ones that you were using just last week or last month, if you want to get technical about it.

Both biologically and developmentally, your toddler self was very different from the infant version of you, and your childhood self didn't much resemble your teenaged self, and so on. The body that you are in at this very moment is significantly different from the one you were using yesterday and also from the one you'll be in tomorrow, on a cellular level. It's a strange concept to be sure, but once you realize that the elements that make up your body are continually dying and being reborn, and that your ideas and beliefs are constantly evolving, you begin to see a basic truth of our humanness: we, ourselves, are synonymous with change.

So why fight it? Historically humans are very good at overcomplicating things, but it truly doesn't have to be that way. Learn to embrace change as inevitable and you might start feeling more relaxed when life throws you those unavoidable curveballs. Plus, answering some of the Big Questions becomes easier when you accept that your answers aren't "one-and-done".

POWER TOOLS:

Now that the pressure is off let's dig deeper into what's important to you in life right now. In order to drill down to the answer, we are going to have some fun with virtual time travel. As you work through these exercises, make sure you're sitting in a quiet place and have a journal handy.

As you read through the prompts, allow your imagination to run wild. The process is about getting in tune with your deepest desires, not about getting caught up in limiting beliefs or in focusing on what you currently do – and do not – have in your life.

You may be living in a one room apartment in a less-than-ideal neighborhood, and be dreaming about sailing a yacht around the Mediterranean, with no idea of how you are going to get from "here" to "there." That's okay. If the yacht thing resonates with you then it means something.

This is going to be a fun adventure into your inner thoughts, so, strap yourself in, and away we go!

Back to the Future: Imagination Activation

Imagine yourself three to five years in the future, painting the most vivid picture you can. Notice where you are and what you are doing. What kind of surroundings are you in? What country or city are you in, or are you out in nature or by the sea? Are you at work, and if so is it a small home office or a large corporate setting? How many people are around you? What do you do or make and how does this make you feel? Try to fully engage all your senses. Get excited about what you're seeing, smelling and tasting, and each time let yourself see and experience more and more details of your perfect world.

It may help to write a description of your ideal life, or to record yourself speaking about your vision. The more you do this the more you'll be able to fine tune and define what you really want. Don't be surprised if certain things come to you very quickly and easily, while others are harder to see. It's not important that you achieve a crystal-clear picture the first time you try this, nor is it important that your vision stays the same every time. What is important is flexing the muscles of your imagination and allowing yourself to have a fully immersive experience. Once you begin to create a clear picture of where you'd like to be in several years it is important to visit this place in your imagination for a few minutes every day.

In today's busy world many people feel that they can't possibly fit even one more thing into their schedules, but this truly is one of the most important steps you'll take on the way to living the life of your dreams. It only takes a few minutes of your time, but should be repeated every day, ideally at the same time of day. You can do it when you first wake up, before you go to sleep, or at some designated time during the day, and you only need to experience your future self in this way for 5-6 minutes in order for this to be effective. And to say that visualization is effective is certainly an understatement.

Successful athletes, actors and speakers use it regularly to great success. Oprah Winfrey frequently talks about her visualization practice and how it not only helped launch her career, landing her a role in The Color Purple when she was an unknown and aspiring actress, but how she continues the practice even today as she grows and transforms her network and other interests. Boxing great Muhammad Ali often talked about how he would visualize the entire fight, including his victory, in his mind before he ever stepped foot in the ring. And Arnold Schwarzenegger is open about how visualization helped him transform himself from a scrawny kid into the legendary bodybuilder, actor and politician that he has become.

While it's true that you must be able to define your goals before you can achieve them, don't worry if the picture of your future self is incomplete. The repetition of this exercise is what makes it so powerful, as is your ability to allow yourself to fully immerse yourself in the experience. When you're driving your dream car, what feelings are you having? Go ahead and really put yourself in that scene, so much so that you allow yourself to experience those feelings now, today. Give yourself permission to feel joy, confidence, satisfaction... whatever it is that you feel when you're in that future picture, invite it in now, for allowing yourself to have those feelings is the quickest way to kick start the transformation of turning your dreams into reality.

And please remember that just because there are things you see your future self having or doing, which you may not have access to today, by no means does that indicate that these things are unattainable or that you "shouldn't" want them. The world is an infinitely abundant place and we all are capable of creating the life that we want, but there is a very definite process to making that happen. This book outlines the steps for you, and you'll find that they're so easy that anyone can do them - but the fact is that very few will. Yes, it's true that we absolutely can have anything our heart desires, but so few of us are willing to step up and claim those gifts. I hope that this book helps you muster the courage to claim what is yours, because it's right there for the taking.

Grounded in the Present: Taking Stock

Now that we've talked about the importance of a daily virtual visit to your future self, we're going to shift focus into the present. Most of us have something about our present situation – or about ourselves – that we'd like to change or work on. Before real change can occur you need to step back and observe where you are right now, at this moment. Don't judge or create stories around why things are the way they are, just take some time to objectively observe the way things are in your life right now. What's working well and giving you joy and satisfaction? In what other areas are you tolerating, but not enjoying, your circumstances?

We've developed a handy checklist to help guide you through the various aspects of your life, from your health to where you live, to your friends and family, hobbies and job. You'll find this list on our website at elinbarton.com/resources, and we recommend going through it when you have 30-60 minutes to sit down and focus on the answers. At this point there is no need to take any action – it is really just about raising your awareness about your life today. Later on we'll talk about developing an action plan using the list, but for now observe without judgment.

As you go through the list you'll find some things on it that will be obvious to you, and others which you hadn't thought about before. You'll probably also find things that are going really well and which are worthy of your gratitude. Raising your awareness around all of it – the good, the bad, and the ugly – is all an important part of the process, so be honest with yourself and if anything does start to come up that you feel the need to journal or explore further, then by all means, do so.

Revisiting the Past: Look but Don't Touch

This chapter is called time shifting but no time shifting would ever be complete without a little jaunt into the past. One thing you should know about the past is, it can be a dangerous place for your psyche. And the other thing is, it's not real. The only place that the past exists is in our imaginations. We all have selective memories to some extent, so our recollections of days gone by are frequently tarnished by the spin we put on them - either seeing things through rose-colored glasses or the lens of doom, neither of which is probably 100% accurate.

Some of us want to forget the past, while others prefer to stay stuck there, replaying the same old movie over and over in their mind, wishing for a different ending that never comes. Well, old movies are fun but the repetition of these stories is neither healthy nor helpful. Whether we're pining over an old romance or remembering someone who hurt us, it is helpful – and healthy - to acknowledge and honor whatever happened, identify the lessons learned, then let it all go.

Some people create a ceremony or ritual around this, writing down old hurts or feelings on bits of paper, then burning them in a glass jar or in a fireplace. The symbolism of seeing those old feelings and experiences literally go up in flames can be very liberating and if you have been feeling stuck it can help you to move on with better energy and more momentum.

No matter what's happened to you, how you've felt betrayed or hurt, or how you've seemingly made mistakes, it's all okay. Really. All of it. Think about it - everything that has ever happened to you has led you up to the point you're at right now. Your life experiences – even experiencing and learning what you don't want - have instilled in you a drive to succeed, which is why you are reading this book and are taking the steps to purposefully build your future.

Looking at the past can also give us perspective and valuable clues about ourselves. It's also a way to gauge where we are on life's journey. In your past you may have had more or less money, a different home or family, a business or another job. You may perceive that your present circumstances are either better or worse than what you experienced in the past, but the truth is, they are just different. Life is a journey with lots of twists and turns in the road. The fact that you'll experience both ups and downs is certain, so you may as well let go of your resistance and enjoy the ride.

Just remember as you move along this road it's best to focus your attention ahead of you. Glance in that rear view mirror from time to time, but turning the car around and going in that direction is not an option. Go ahead and look back if you'd like, but don't get stuck in what would/ should/ could have happened. Stick to the facts and focus forward. Enjoy the good memories and learn the lessons that need to be learned, then move on. The ability to do this will not only make you a more agile time shifter – it will also serve you well as you carve out the future that you most deeply desire.

PAGE OF REFLECTION

Affirmation: *I give myself permission to change, grow and evolve*

Time Traveling Debrief

How did you feel going through the time traveling exercises? What came up for you?

How does it feel to look at your future self? What excites you most about that picture?

What was the most surprising thing that you found you're tolerating in your present world? What are you going to do about it?

Were you able to identify some beliefs you're holding onto that are no longer serving you?

When you think about the fact that change is inevitable, how does it make you feel? What came up for you when you were reading that section?

What other new ideas came up during these exercises?

CHAPTER 6
The Money Myth

*"If I had a million dollars I'd buy you some art (a Picasso
or a Garfunkel)... If I had a million dollars I'd buy you a
fur coat (but not a real fur coat, that's cruel)... If I had a
million dollars I'd be rich."*
-Barenaked Ladies

*"Money, get away; Get a good job with good pay
and you're okay
Money, it's a gas; Grab that cash with both hands
and make a stash
New car, caviar, four-star daydream;
Think I'll buy me a football team"*
-Roger Waters

Money is such an interesting topic for me. Most people want more of it, yet in and of itself it has no real value unless it's being circulated and traded for something else. We could argue that the miser who has millions of dollars but never spends a cent is not wealthy in most senses of the word. He or she is certainly not truly living a life of abundance if their main objective is to simply hoard and keep more and more money.

To be of any real value, money must be allowed to flow.

For many people money can have negative connotations. It can cause extreme stress, destroy marriages and obliterate friendships. People go to war for it and many a family has experienced tension or even estrangement over loans gone bad or the disbursement of a deceased relative's assets.

Money is an emotionally charged topic and it's easy to harbor the illusion that having more of it automatically leads to more happiness. However, it's not hard to find evidence that this is far from the truth if you simply study what happens to most people after a lottery win or other windfall. Rather than leading to "happily ever after," those situations frequently result in new stress, broken friendships, shattered relationships and the loss of even more astronomical amounts of money in a very short period of time.

Yet, money is neutral; meaning it's neither good nor evil. It's okay to want it and to have it. It's smart to honor money and use it wisely, but it's of no use to anyone – including yourself – if you never allow anything pleasurable to come from it. Money needs to be respected and valued. It wants to be cultivated and tended to as you would a prized garden. Love it, care for it and when you use it to pay for something, take the time to really appreciate the goods or service that you're receiving as part of the exchange.

So, what does that mean? Should we stop working for money, stop wanting it? Absolve ourselves of the desire for material things in lieu of some higher calling? You may be relieved to know that none of that will be necessary and that living in true abundance means having both a comfortable lifestyle and finding meaningful and fulfilling ways to make a positive impact.

It's easy to be magnanimous about money when you have it, but when you're struggling to make ends meet it can be a challenge to keep an abundance mindset about money. I mean, the pressures add up quickly. Bill collectors can be relentless and even little things, like having your debit card rejected when you're in the checkout at the supermarket, can feel like a blow to your very soul.

Having been on both sides of the fence, I can affirm that having money is a whole lot more fun than being broke. But when you are scraping the bottom of the proverbial barrel the only way out is to trick yourself into thinking that you're living in abundance. It might sound a little cuckoo, but trust me, if you're living in a mentality of "lack," focusing on what you do not have, you're just going to keep attracting more of that same lack.

Don't Worry, Be Happy

If you do find yourself with a shortage of funds or with a big looming debt then what you've got to do is first and foremost, stop making money and bills the things that suck most of your attention and energy. You must find a way to both deal with your responsibilities AND keep enjoying life. It cannot be either/or, or you'll stay stuck in an endless loop that feeds back messages of lack to you again and again.

Money can seem like a really big deal, but in reality, it is nothing more than energy. If you want more of it a good place to start is by releasing any tension you are holding onto around this topic.

Just like the other principles we've addressed in this book, money will flow in and it will flow out. If you can accept that whatever part of the cycle you're in with money is temporary then it might make it easier to get through some of the tough times. In researching this book, I talked with plenty of people who have made and lost millions time and time again. Losing a large amount of money is no fun, but it is not the end of the world. Money can come to you in so many different ways but how quickly and easily this will happen is directly tied to your mindset.

You've Got to Give a Little

You can love money and still give it away. In fact, even if you just have a little money, giving some of it away is a sure-fire way to attract more money to you. The simple act of giving is saying to the Universe, "I believe in abundance and know that anything I give will come back to me in multiples."

Some people are meticulously consistent about tithing or donating 10% of anything they make to a church or other non-profit. Whether you decide to tithe or come up with your own methodology, I highly recommend you find a way to either do the same or regularly donate to a cause you care about. Pay it forward the next time you're in Starbucks or the grocery store. Leave your waitress an overly generous tip. Round up your grocery bill to give to the food pantry. Do these things even if you feel like you can't really afford it, because one of the curious things I've found about money is that the more you allow it to flow, the more generous you are with it and the more you give it gladly with an open heart, the more it comes back to you.

If you feel like you're drowning in debt and can't afford it, you're still wealthier than more than half of the people on this planet, so give anyway. Even if it's a few pennies or dollars, find a way to donate something. Not only does giving feel good and empowering, a funny thing happens when you start to do this. You'll begin to see more money and wealth come back to you, often in unexpected ways.

Money is a Great Teacher

One of the interesting things about not having money is that you will find out very quickly who your true supporters are. Oprah has a quote about how, when you're successful, everyone queues up to ride with you in the limo. But when you're struggling and on the proverbial "back of the bus" only your true friends will be back there with you. Because money does come and go, and because you don't have to stay in a struggling state forever (unless you choose to do so), please don't forget those people who were kind to you and who treated you with respect when you had nothing. Notice who those people were and keep them in your inner circle. Then pay it forward and help someone else with your own kindness, compassion and generosity.

> *"It's good to have money and the things that money can buy, but it's good too, to check up once in a while and make sure that you haven't lost the things that money can't buy."*
> **-George Lorimer**

In many ways, not always having free and easy access to money is a great opportunity to learn about ourselves, our own resourcefulness and about our ability to be truly grateful. It's also one way we can learn real empathy for others. When we don't have money it's also an opportunity to use, recognize, and share the many gifts and great abundance that are already surrounding us.

I can't tell you how many stories I've heard about people achieving the greatest happiness and peace when they had very little in terms of material goods. We all have so many blessings that are surrounding us when we take the time to really look and see what's there. Instead of giving a physical gift to someone you may find yourself giving of yourself, your time, or your creativity. There can be a lot of true blessings that emerge from those situations, so if you do find yourself in a place of lack try shifting your perspective to a place of gratitude. By doing that you'll often find that money once again begins to flow to you.

When you learn to relax your energy around money, you actually open yourself up energetically to receiving more wealth. It's a counterintuitive concept, I know, but one that I've seen put into practice time and time again. Learn to welcome abundance into your life without making money your only motivator. Also, learn to recognize that we think that we want money because we believe it's going to make us feel a certain way. But – plot twist – since we each control our feelings we can choose to feel that way now, before the money shows up.

POWER TOOL - Practice experiencing the feeling of love, confidence, happiness and abundance NOW to immediately start attracting more of it into your life.

MONEY MYTHS – Let's explore some of the most common misconceptions people have about money. Which of these resonate with you, and what will it take to let go of the belief?

1. Poof! Let me wave my magic wand.

One of the most important misconceptions is that money in and of itself will make you happy and will turn you, as if by magic, into a different person. This one is a big fat "false". No way. That is never, ever going to be the case.

Having money (or not having money) is simply a state of being. It does not change who you are at a core level. When you have a strong sense of self, whether you have money or not is, in some ways, as inconsequential as whether you're wearing your pajamas or jeans and a t-shirt. Sure, you might look a little different or be heading to a different place. You might have different priorities and intentions, but you're still the same at your core.

However, that said, much of what you probably want more of in your life – friends, family, adventure – are things that you can start working on right now, regardless of the number that is reflected in your bank account. Remember, that number will change. Fortunes are made and lost every day. Focus on figuring out who you are and what you stand for because ultimately that is what really matters.

If you are planning on having more money at your disposal in the near future, and I sincerely hope that you are, you can speed the process along by starting to prepare for that day. Learn about money and investing. Find out what kind of account you're going to have to keep your money in. Get educated. Find a trustworthy financial planner and start talking to them about your goals. Find out what you can do now to change your spending and saving habits, and then start doing it. If you don't have discipline and get savvy around money now, don't expect to automatically receive those skills when your fortune does show up. Set yourself up for success by making changes now that will serve you well in the long term.

2. Money is evil, bad, etc.

See Myth #1.

Money never "makes" a person good or bad. In fact, taken by itself it is nothing more than an abstract concept. Much of the time these days, we aren't even talking about pieces of paper when we refer to money. Most of our money and wealth is only ever counted virtually – numbers on a computer screen. And that becomes even more relevant as currencies like Bitcoin become more mainstream.

Money is a tool; nothing more, nothing less. We don't need to get all emotionally charged around the subject. And yes, people do sometimes do unscrupulous and ugly things because of money, but those actions are under the control of the individuals involved – the money itself is a completely neutral entity. There is nothing wrong with wanting and acquiring money. It's necessary in our world today and having access to it means that you also have more resources to enjoy life and do good in the world.

3. Eyes wide open.

It is, for some of us, a challenge to take a good hard look at our finances, or to get educated about money, investments and savings. Many people have an aversion to these topics and get physically (and mentally) uncomfortable when they are brought up in conversation. Early on in my business I was working with a coach who advised me to look at my business books with curiosity, and without any judgment.

"They are just numbers," she told me. "What are they saying to you? What are they revealing? What patterns do you see emerging and how can you use that information?"

It's hard to admit, but in the early days of my business, even as I was being coached, I couldn't do it. I hated looking at my numbers. I felt like they weren't good enough, and that therefore I wasn't good enough, and it was easier for me to play the "ostrich" role and hope for the best.

My method of "pretend it's not happening" was not sustainable and eventually I had to get over my limiting thoughts, but it wasn't easy.

Whether you're running a business or doing your own personal accounting, tuning into your finances, being aware of how much you have, how much you need and what things cost, is absolutely necessary. In that way, you can take better care of the money you already have and prepare for more to come in the future.

And the price for not being prepared can be very high. I've seen it again and again; people come into some amount of money through any number of sources – an inheritance, court settlement, bonus at work – and then quickly (or over time) end up squandering the money away due to a lack of education, attention and planning. So, what I say is, whether you're starting a new venture, improving an existing one or just looking at tweaking your current situation and making it better, take some time to learn about money, investing and finance. If you don't already have a budget, go ahead and make one. Find out how much you need monthly and annually to meet your basic expenses and how much it will take to lead the life you truly desire. Really research what it's going to take to live your dream life and put a number to it. Believe that it's possible to reach that number, as mindset is the first step towards finding success with money.

If your numbers aren't currently where you'd like them to be, then at least be aware of how big the gap is. What can you start doing today to get yourself closer to that number? Remember I said that you don't need to know every step of your journey to the life of your dreams, and that is true, but you do need to keep moving in the right general direction of where you'll want to go. Your actions help keep you focused around your goals and at the same time send a strong message to the Universe that you're serious about improving your money situation. Know your numbers. Own them. And let go of emotional attachment around where you are right now with money. The only way you'll ever be able to change your situation is first by seeing where you are and where you're going.

Sometimes people create a vacation or "splurge" fund when they decide to forgo their daily coffee shop stop or restaurant lunches. You'd be surprised by how quickly five dollars here and there can add up. But in addition to the money you're saving, when you start developing habits like these you also begin to see money show up in your life in new and unexpected ways.

4. Earning or attracting money is hard.

If you've ever had this thought, please erase it right now.

The idea that you can only earn a certain number of dollars per hour, and only qualify for a certain salary level throughout the life of your career is outdated. Moreover, it puts unfortunate limiting thoughts on the whole idea of abundance. If you've studied any Law of Attraction teachings you know that one of the central themes is that we live in an abundant Universe of unlimited potential, and that the only limits are those that originate in our own imaginations. So, let's start shifting these thoughts right now. While your current situation may involve an hourly wage, that certainly does not need to be your reality forevermore.

Money comes easily to plenty of people who are not as smart, good looking or charming as yourself, and it does so every single minute of every day. There is no reason that you can't tap into that flow using your special gifts, and in a way that will work with your situation. Sounds good, right? There are just a couple of things you need to know. The first one is that the more you are able to align with your purpose – by using your core gifts to serve the greater good – the easier this actually is. You'll find that when you're really tuned into that purpose the Universe will conspire to put the right people in your path and you'll move forward in creating what you really want much faster and easier than you ever could have imagined.

The thing to keep in mind is, although the Universe will help you, it doesn't mean that there isn't any work involved. In fact, building a business or a dream career usually involves a great deal of dedicated, focused, diligent, "pedal to the metal" hard, hard work.

Visualization is a powerful tool, but sitting around just thinking about your dream will never make it happen for you. You have to actually do the work, and that is what the "grit" part of this book is all about. When you're working in alignment with your passion and your purpose you will find that much of the work feels invigorating and fun. It's a great adrenaline rush to create something that you really believe in, and when you're working within this kind of energy you open up opportunities for all kinds of magic to happen – magic that you activate by showing up and doing your part.

5. Focus on abundance, not lack.

When you don't have money in your life, or when you don't have enough money, it's very easy to get caught up in feeling poor, inadequate, or even panicky when you can't pay your bills. How many of us have woken up in the middle of the night in a cold sweat, wondering how we're going to make ends meet? This state of fear around money is understandable, but it's not helpful on any level, so go ahead – take a deep breath and release that emotional baggage.

When you're in panic mode you are not thinking clearly or strategically. And you're probably not giving off energy that inspires any kind of confidence in you or your work. Although most people aren't consciously aware of it, when you walk into a room your energy is "introducing" you to others before you ever say a single word. One of the coaches I have worked with told me that he so strongly believes in this phenomenon that before he goes on a sales call, even if he very much needs to make the sale, he works on his energy before ever getting out of the car.

He told me once, "If the other person ever senses desperation or that I need them more than they need me, it's all over. I play a game with myself of acting as if I am at the pinnacle of success even if I'm having a bad month. Changing my mindset and energy and mimicking someone who is super successful is the fastest way to attract success."

Another one of my sales friends says that she imagines bathing the room with a warm light before she goes into any business meeting. She consciously sets the intention for a positive outcome and finds that ends up being the case most of the time.

> *When you are grateful fear disappears and*
> *abundance appears.*
> -**Tony Robbins**

One of the quickest ways to get yourself out of a state of fear around money is to take note of all the good that you have in your life and to get yourself to a place of gratitude around those things. Take care of what you already have in the best way that you can. You may not have the newest, fanciest model of car but you can keep your car clean and tidy and well-maintained.

You may not live in anything resembling a mansion, but you can keep your apartment or house neat and nicely decorated. There are plenty of ideas online for creative ways to upcycle or reuse items, so having a comfortable and pleasant living space is not something that you have to put off doing until you have more money. I recall the people who lived across the street from us in California. This family didn't have a lot of money, but they were hard workers. Their house was small and provided very tight quarters for two parents and three growing children. Their home could easily have been in a perpetual state of chaos but in fact, that was never the case.

Not only was their home spotless but they had taken the time to decorate and furnish it with care and creativity. They were expert up-cyclers and that little house was both welcoming and adorable. The family took meticulous care of the house for years, then out of the blue a series of events unfolded (that's the Universe for you) that led them to move to a much bigger and better house. Once they moved they filled their new house with the same gratitude and grace and made it just as homey and comfortable as their last place.

They were ready for real abundance when the opportunity presented itself because they had already been practicing an abundant lifestyle for years. Remember, money doesn't make you into the person you want to be – you have to become that person first, so you're prepared when the money does come.

6. Own any past mistakes or debts. And own your current spending habits.

Many people get caught up in debt and end up focusing a great deal of their attention on a stressful situation that was created from past circumstances. This, however, is not a helpful place to put your attention when you're wanting to create something new, but there are ways to deal with old debt and to move forward effectively.

First, you need to own the fact that you have the debt. If you're avoiding taking calls from bill collectors, or if you are trying not to talk to people who you owe money to, just stop. Pick up the phone and make the calls. Explain your situation and try to arrange a payment. Figure out your current minimum living expenses then add in 10% for miscellaneous expenses and 10% for savings. On top of that give yourself another 10% for fun money. You have to keep living, even while getting out of debt.

Once you've done those calculations the amount that's left is what you can spend on your creditors each month. Divide that up among them and set up automatic payments so you don't have to focus your attention and energy on the old debt. Pay more towards the old debt when you can but make sure your focus is on the future, not on the past. Even if you can only afford to pay a few dollars a month, you're moving in the right direction and you're freeing up your energy to focus on new opportunities.

Saving money is a foreign concept to many people these days, especially if you already feel like you're being stretched to the limit. Try to get in the habit of saving 10% of what you earn and be strict about this. There are plenty of apps that will help you do this automatically, and if you set one of those up, you'll be more likely to be successful. Remember, you have to own the whole situation with your money, whether you're just starting out or whether you're recovering from old mistakes, but this does not have to be an unpleasant experience. So many people get emotionally stressed about money, but you, my friend, do not have to be one of them because now you clearly see that money is a tool that can help you not only achieve your own dreams, but also do great good in the world around you.

PAGE OF REFLECTION

Dear Money...

This exercise might seem a little strange, but it's incredibly effective.

You're going to write a letter to Money and you're going to explore your feelings around this topic. You might need to apologize to Money for squandering it in the past, or for not being grateful enough for its presence in your life.

You might need to really explore that gratitude angle and write in detail about all the things and opportunities that Money has provided for you.

Get as detailed as you like, and have fun with this as it's an impactful exercise that will uncover some of your underlying beliefs around money. If you discover that you don't trust money or even like it very much, you may need to work on these core beliefs before riches can come flowing into your life.

Maybe it's not the money that's holding you back.

It's easy to make money the scapegoat, but what if it's not actually what's holding you back? If you are looking to receive an abundance of money it's important to prepare to accept those riches when they come, but many people don't have a clue where to start.

In this exercise, take these amounts of money one by one and write down in detail how you're going to spend every penny – and yes, you have to spend all of it each time. The more detailed you are the better – itemize exact dollar amounts, the make, model and exact cost of things you want to buy, etc.

$5,000

$50,000

$500,000

$5,000,000

$50,000,000

What new ideas came up during these exercises?

CHAPTER 7
Finding Your Tribe

You are the average of the five people you spend the most time with – including yourself.
-Jim Rohn

Surround yourself with only people who are going to lift you higher.
-Oprah Winfrey

You may have heard it said that there is the family we are born into and then that other family that we choose. Some people call that chosen inner circle "framily" – friends who are so close to you that they're like family. Oftentimes these people end up being even closer to you than your actual blood relatives. And the thing is, whether you're building a business or a life it is critically important to consciously surround yourself with a network of people who really do have your back.

The people in our lives play many different roles, and the intention of this chapter is to focus in on your relationships as they relate to you building your business or your dream. Through this narrow lens we're going to take a strategic approach to building your tribe.

And by the way, you might have great friends and family members, but that alone doesn't get them admission to this club. There may be plenty of compelling reasons that you intentionally choose NOT to allow close friends or family members into this inner "dream" circle.

When you're serious about chasing a dream, you're going to need to acquire certain skills and you're going to have to grow your professional network. You'll be well-served by finding an experienced mentor or coach, or by joining a "mastermind" group of people who are already successful or who have expertise in an area that you need to know about.

So, how do you go about connecting with the right people to connect with? Well, to start with you have to first determine where your own strengths and weaknesses lie. There are plenty of inexpensive or free resources for people who are getting started in business and who are looking to learn basic principles and skills. I highly recommend that you take advantage of these so that you can understand the day-to-day operations and make informed decisions.

When you're looking for people to bring into your inner circle you shouldn't necessarily be bringing someone in just because they can teach you how to balance your books or run a marketing campaign. Instead, try seeking out people who are experienced in the field you want to break into; people who can help provide support and valuable insight when you're faced with challenges. This support can be practical – in terms of advice or resources – and it can also be emotional. Your journey is going to be more successful and more fun if you take the time to build this tribe, so carefully consider who you're going to invite inside.

Purposefully expanding that network by design, not by chance, is an interesting exercise. Start out by making a wish list of attributes you'd like to see in your tribe members. Some people like to assign a number to each attribute – just list them out, number one through however many items are on your list.

Then make a list of people who are already in your network, or who you think you could be introduced to by a friend. Next to each person's name write the numbers of the attributes you think they have. The people who check the most boxes are the ones to approach first about being one of your advisers.

Here are some additional questions you may wish to consider when forming this group:

- What type of people do you want to be spending your time with?

- Who is the most likely to support you and raise you up?

- Who is most likely to help you achieve your goals for the right reasons (because they understand your vision and want to see you achieve whatever it is you're setting out to do)?

- Who is most likely to cheer you on when times get tough?

- Who has a sense of humor and is going to make you see the funny side of things during times of struggle?

- Who can be a critical thinker and ask tough questions while not putting you or your ideas down? Who can sit with you and help you dream?

- Who can encourage you to dream bigger, to be stronger?

- And finally, who is going to be that person that is going to call you out when you don't do the things you said you were going to do?

Once you figure out who you'd like to ask to join your tribe, reach out one by one with a personal message, card or phone call. Tell them what you want to create and why you chose them to be one of your inner circle. Be authentic, humble and do not, under any circumstances, get offended if they turn you down. If that happens it does not mean that your idea is bad or that you did anything wrong. It probably just means that they're busy and can't allocate the time right now. Such is life. Move on and ask someone else.

On that note, when people do say yes, be very clear about how much time you are asking for and be very respectful of however much time they agree to give you. Creating a tribe or group of advisers can make a world of difference for your endeavor, but each of those tribe members have their own responsibilities and interests to attend to. Please keep that in mind and remember to always be grateful and gracious whenever they share their time and ideas with you.

And on the other side of that coin...

An equally important question, in addition to who do you want in your tribe, is who do you currently have in your "framily" that you might need to create a little distance from?

You don't necessarily have to break off any of your relationships but do be wary of letting negative people too close to your dream. There are people who will sap the bulk of your energy and they're the same ones who are quick to let you know all the ways in which you're bound to fail.

Because your mindset is so important when it comes to your success, the importance of protecting your headspace and your energy really cannot be overstated. With the right people supporting you your growth will be greatly accelerated, but the Negative Nellies need a swift kick out of that inner circle of yours.

Incidentally, I am not saying that everyone around you has to support you with blind faith and Pollyanna-ish enthusiasm. Someone who plays devil's advocate or asks tough questions can be a very important asset as you build. What you don't need, however, is the "Debbie downer" – that person who is convinced you're going to fail and loves telling you about how bad things are at every possible opportunity. It's that type of negative person who can really mess with your mojo when you're looking to make a big change in your life.

But what happens if you're married to one of those negative people? What if I'm describing your mom? Or your best friend? What do you do if all your friends are like that? Honestly, if that was the case you might want to look at finding some new friends. Even if it's someone like a parent or a spouse, who you do want to stay connected to, you do need to come up with ground rules around how you talk about this thing that you're building, or perhaps that entire subject is taboo. Whatever rules you set, make sure you tell the other person, so they are aware that the rules exist. And then enforce those rules without exception. Remember, it's in everyone's best interest to keep the energetic path to your success as clear as possible.

Building Your Inner Circle

"Every mind needs friendly contact with other minds, for food of expansion and growth."
- **Napoleon Hill**

"Surround yourself with people who are smarter than you."
-**Russell Simmons**

If you think of your network as a series of concentric circles with yourself at the core, consider who you want right by your side. Who is most likely to be your biggest and strongest support? These people might already be in your network and maybe they are the people who really "get" what you're doing. They've got your back. You can talk freely with them about any challenges or problems that come up. And these are the people that won't judge when that happens, but will help you with problem solving, while continuing to be your cheerleaders. Choose these people wisely and you'll be stacking the odds of success dramatically in your favor.

The people who are closest to the core and essence of your dream might be people you already know, or perhaps you haven't met them yet. They may be people in your community who you admire or a friend of a friend who is good at business. Identify people who you would most like to help you, then ask. In a world where everyone is busy, some of the people who you do ask will probably decline. Don't worry about it. Focus on finding a few good people who are going to be a devoted support team for what you're looking to grow. There are different ways to structure your inner circle, and anywhere from one to six people on the inside will do very nicely to start. Here are three different ways you can leverage your core support team effectively.

The Mastermind Group

Napoleon Hill is credited with coming up with the idea of the mastermind group and he has discussed the subject in several of his books, including *Think and Grow Rich* and *The Law of Success*. And while mastermind groups can be structured in a variety of ways, most of the most successful ones have between 4-12 dedicated members and a regular time to meet. The group has to set its own rules, but many successful groups take turns letting one member have the "spotlight" for a certain amount of time during the meeting where that person presents a question or challenge that he or she has been experiencing to the group. The group members then brainstorm solutions for that "spotlight" member. Sometimes that can take up the whole meeting, or the group might choose to allocate only a certain amount of time to the spotlight segment, then allow 10-15 minutes for each of the other members to be "laser coached" by the group on some topic. In the way of a true mastermind group, every member gets to take something of value away from the meeting.

A Mentor or Advisory Board

An alternative to forming a mastermind in that inner circle is to set up a similar group that functions as a board or advisory council or to find a single person to work with you as a mentor.

One of the major differences between this type of group (or mentor) and the mastermind is that the focus of the meetings is always on you and your project or business, whereas in a mastermind all the group members take turns being coached. Ultimately people who sit on boards for businesses are frequently paid for their time, but when you're starting out you may be able to find people who will help you because they believe in what you're doing. If you're able to inspire that kind of confidence and dedication from others you are off to a great start. Remember, if you are asking people to donate their time and possibly other resources, please be sure to thank them profusely and to honor and respect what they're giving to you.

What I mean by this, is this is the time to tap deep into your gratitude and, if you can, to offer to buy your advisors coffee or lunch in exchange for their dedicated attention or help.

These advisors or mentors are offering you their expertise more as teachers than as the give-and-take of the mastermind group, so make sure you let them know how much you appreciate it. Come to your meetings prepared with questions, problems and progress reports. You will be much more likely to find people who will mentor and advise you if you are willing to show that you're the type of person who will step up and do the work. Most people like to help others, but in a world where everyone is so busy, if your mentor feels like he or she isn't being heard or isn't making an impact, don't expect the relationship to last very long.

Accountability Partner

An alternative to a mastermind group or a mentor or advisory board is to find yourself an accountability partner. Oftentimes this will be someone else who is also building their dream, and you can help one another by meeting up regularly and sharing your progress with one another. At every meeting you each state some actions that you're going to take before the next meeting. Then, at the beginning of the next meeting or sometime in between meetings you report back about the thing that you said you were going to do.

There is something powerful about having a partner who you have to report to and a deadline which you have to finish something by to help keep momentum going. People frequently find that without this type of self-imposed structure and accountability, life too frequently "gets in the way" and the steps that need to happen to propel you towards your dreams get pushed back in lieu of other responsibilities. But that dream is important and when you take the time to create and nurture your inner circle very intentionally you are sending a very clear signal that you're serious about being successful in the creation of whatever it is you've been dreaming of.

Your Wider Network: Bigger Circles

*The two most powerful words when we're
in struggle? Me too!*
-**Brene Brown**

*If you want to go fast go alone.
If you want to go far go together.*
-**African proverb**

The next layer of circles in your networks is also important to your success and warrants some discussion. While these people are not privy to the same level of intimate detail that the first group is, they are still an important component to your ultimate success. These are people who you may know socially or in a business setting and who you need to start talking about your dream to. The more you can articulate your vision and commit publicly to what you're creating, the more likely you are to actually make it happen.

Writing this book has been a long-time dream of mine, but it's one that has been on the back burner for many years as I focused on my family and raising my kids while running a busy production company. It was only when I started talking about this book publicly, putting a date on when it was going to be released, that I knew it would actually happen. Giving myself a deadline seemed to send a very clear message to the Universe. I had committed to a publication date but putting it in my bio on my website and in my blog posts really accelerated my actions and helped ensure I really got the job done.

It was scary to publicly state a publication date before the book was even finished but interestingly, once I did that, the right people started showing up in my path. At an event I attended I was asked by near strangers to join a mastermind group, and that group has turned out to be a strong support for this project. I also was introduced to my publisher, as well as a myriad of others who have formed an informal editorial board for me. The list of acknowledgments is already long, and it continues to grow, but no one would ever have known that I had the book dream if I hadn't started talking about it.

Sharing a dream before it's come to fruition, sometimes before the idea is even fully formed, can be totally intimidating. It puts you in a place of vulnerability, especially if you start telling those negative people we were talking about at the beginning of this chapter.

So, while you do have to share with some discretion, it is important to make the leap of faith and declare what you are doing. The more you talk about it, actually, the more real it will start to seem. Of course, talk alone is not enough to make things happen for you, which is why the "Grit" part of this book is probably the most important section. But you will be much more likely to find success if you properly prepare for it, and part of that process does involve creating this network for yourself and also setting up some public accountability. Stating a timeline, like I did when I announced when this book was coming out, gives you a place of reference to work backwards from, and in that way you can almost reverse engineer that thing you are creating.

And who exactly should you be talking to in these next levels of people? Well, this too is by design. These are more of your family and friends, but you also need to begin putting yourself in situations where you are most likely to meet people who can help support you. If you aspire to be an artist, then you should find a way to get to know other artists and also people who buy art (assuming your intention is to sell your work). Begin attending events and seek out opportunities to go to workshops or other educational forums and seminars. The internet is a plethora of information and people do meet one another and form real friendships there, but there really is something to be said for getting out and talking to people face to face too. Get out of your comfort zone, go to events. Meet new people. Talk to people when you're standing in line at the supermarket, strike up conversations. When you start telling people what you're up to you'll probably find that you'll get suggestions like, "Oh, you really need to talk to so-and-so..."

When that happens, follow those "breadcrumbs" because a lot of times that is the exact way the Universe shows up to guide you along your path. Start taking the attitude that no one is put into your path by chance, that everyone is either a blessing or a lesson. Be curious and allow yourself to be vulnerable. You never know who is going to help you get where you want to go, and you'll never find out if you don't start talking to people about what you're doing.

PAGE OF REFLECTION

Affirmation: *I am building a network of supporters to accelerate my success.*

Your imaginary board

In this chapter you were given a lot of information about assembling your advisers and close tribe of supporters.

Now, imagine you could have anyone from all of history on your board of advisers. Choose five or six people - living or dead – and "ask" them to be on your board. Close your eyes and imagine they are in the room with you, ready to counsel you on any issue. Meditate for a few minutes, going one by one through the roster of this imaginary board. What does each of these people have to tell you? What advice would they give?

Become a Networking Superstar

Networking – both in person and online – is a great way to meet new people and establish new relationships. Keep in mind that no matter where you're networking a good rule of thumb is to go into the situation not thinking about what you can get from the other person but asking how you can be of service.

Try to strike up meaningful conversation and listen attentively to the answers. Do not go directly into your sales pitch. You can talk about your company in an informative way without being too salesy.

Your conversations don't need to be long, but they do need to be meaningful on some level or else you're wasting your time.

Plan for Success

Do some research to find out where good networking opportunities might be. LinkedIn can be a good place online to meet other professionals. If you're going to use that platform make sure your profile and picture are up to date, and remember, building your network with real connections is a long game and will not happen overnight. Still, the payoff for many business owners is substantial if they are willing to put in the required time.

In person networking events can be hit-or-miss. Practice your short (30 second) and long (2 minute) elevator pitch. Make sure it gives a clear, concise and memorable summary of your services, as well as one piece of information about the types of people you'd like to get connected to.

Get a hold of a calendar – either a physical planner or a digital version – and set a goal for daily (probably online) and weekly networking quotas. Put it right into your schedule and when the time comes, just do it.

Make sure follow up becomes part of your routine, too. Relationships are rarely built on a single meeting. Remember, it's about making authentic connections.

What new ideas came up during these exercises?

CHAPTER 8
Expect the Best

"In order to carry a positive action, we must develop here a positive vision."
-Dalai Lama

We are shaped by our thoughts; we become what we think. When the mind is pure, joy follows like a shadow that never leaves.
-Buddha

"I just don't want to get my hopes up," Katrina said, staring down into her Caesar salad. "I mean, I think this is a really good idea, but I don't want to be disappointed."

Wait, what? Moments ago she was super excited about her new endeavor, and then suddenly, as if something inside her brain went "snap", she talked herself out of even trying.

Have you ever seen someone do this, or perhaps have done it yourself?

That type of thinking does one thing and one thing only: sets you up for failure. It's a defense mechanism that is woven so tightly in the human psyche that many of us have probably been carrying this tendency for decades, where it was embedded after being carried by generations of our ancestors. This ability to talk ourselves out of something that we actually really want is so deep that it's become part of our very DNA.

Remember, just because it's deep and raw and real doesn't mean that we can't change our way of thinking.

And boy oh boy, getting rid of those old limiting thoughts is one of the most important things that you can do to ensure your future successes.

Gabi is in the middle of a big struggle with money. She is moving into a new apartment, recently got into a car accident and needed emergency surgery. By her estimation she had a deficit of $4,000-$5,000 and this was causing her a great deal of stress. She couldn't see any solution to her problem, yet as she was telling the story she also shared, as a side note, that several people actually owed her money and that she was in line for a promotion at work.

It seemed obvious that at least part of the solution to Gabi's problem was well within her grasp, yet she was so focused on a negative outcome that she couldn't even see how realistic, if not likely, a successful resolution was.

Gabi was so caught up in fear and doubt that it was like she was wearing blinders. She just couldn't see opportunities that were right in front of her.

How many times have we created the exact same kind of self-sabotage for ourselves?

Plenty of research has been done into how expectations affect outcomes. Teachers and parents who expect children to excel, and who demonstrate absolute faith in that student, very frequently get the results they expect – which is to say, excellence.

By the same token, teachers who expect their students to be unruly or to fail academically frequently find that the experience they have matches exactly what they were expecting, too.

I'm not saying that teachers are solely responsible for the behavior of students. But there is a direct correlation between the results you are expecting and what you actually get to experience.

This same philosophy extends to all aspects of your life. If you have certain standards, and expect a certain lifestyle or level of income, chances are that you are going to find a way to achieve that, as long as you don't lose your focus and your belief that it's possible or required.

That faith component is really a big part of the key to this whole thing. I have a friend who has not always had an easy life, but who has always had certain standards about what type of lifestyle she considers to be acceptable for herself. My friend is a hard worker and is not snobbish by any means, but I can guarantee that even if her money and possessions were to disappear overnight, she would maintain certain standards.

For example, she would present herself to the world in a very beautiful, well put together package. My friend is unlikely to ever eat a package of ramen noodles or canned spaghetti. No, it's fresh organic fruit and vegetables for her. She expects to be treated and taken care of in a certain way, and for the most part people respond to those expectations.

The standards you set for what you will or will not tolerate are critical to the type of experience you are going to have. If you expect that you will have plenty of resources, somehow those resources will find you. If you expect that you'll have transportation, friends, food, whatever it is that you desire, one way or another those things will make their way to you.

If you expect things to work out, for rewards to come, AND if you do the work that's required to propel you on that journey, I have no doubt that it will happen for you. Why would it not, and why would you expect anything less?

And as you learn to be intentional about what you are willing to tolerate, you can also become sure about what you expect to show up in your life. Several years ago my sister was a young single mom of twins and a new teacher in a Waldorf school. She had little time and money and her car was literally falling apart. The time for its inspection was coming up and she knew that it wasn't going to pass. She lived out in the country and there was no way to get to town or to work without a car, and she didn't have the resources to replace the one she had.

Our family was concerned about her, but we lived across the country and at the time none of us had the means to contribute much to her either, certainly not enough to buy a new car. Instead of getting all worked up about it, my sister announced to us all that we shouldn't worry; she was going to manifest a car.

I have to admit that we all were skeptical that this was going to happen, but wouldn't you know, a couple of weeks later one of the families at the school wanted to donate their car to the school and because the school didn't have an immediate need for a vehicle they offered it to my sister on an indefinite loan.

The way that the car came to her just when she needed it almost seemed like magic, yet miracles like that happen every single day to people who state what they want or need, fully expect it to show up and who are open to "how" this is going to happen. Sometimes these gifts or opportunities will come about in unconventional, even unbelievable ways, but that's what happens when you act and live in faith that the Universe is conspiring for you.

This "leap of faith" is required for your dreams to truly come to pass.

Does this mean you can sit around wishing for a new car and one will magically appear in your driveway? No, of course not. However, if you need or want something bad enough and if you truly believe and feel that it is already yours, the pieces of the puzzle have an uncanny habit of falling into place.

The tricky part to this is, you have to believe that you're receiving whatever it is you want before you actually get it. You have to feel deep gratitude because you're gotten it. Drink in the experience of the gifts you've received and experience them fully.

This can be difficult if your present circumstances are not currently good. You may be struggling financially, feeling stuck in a job or other circumstance, or you may be involved in an unhealthy relationship. You might have no idea how in the world you are going to get from where you are presently to where you really want to be – whatever that definition of wild success means to you.

And listing off all the obstacles – all the reasons why the dream could never happen for you – well, that would be very, very easy. I'm sure if I asked you, you could rattle off those reasons without even thinking very much about this at all. "My dream is doomed to fail because I'm not smart enough, I don't have enough money, someone is already doing this, I should have started 20 years ago... "

The excuses are endless once we get going, but remember, we get what we focus on, so if you spend all your time thinking of the reasons you couldn't possibly succeed, well, guess what. Your chances of success are going downhill with every single reason you voice for why you can't do something. So, I implore you, please stop now. No more excuses and no more focusing on the worst possible outcome. Sure, you might try something and you might not succeed the first time or the second time or the tenth time, but if you never try your chances of success are much closer to zero than anyone who is brave enough to at least give it a shot.

I recently interviewed a man who developed a game called Color Switch that was, for some time, the number one downloaded app worldwide. In fact, this app ended up with more than 150 million downloads and David's company made millions of dollars.

And yet, this man, David Reichelt, had zero app design or programming experience until just a few short years ago. In fact, at that time he was $80,000 in debt and working several odd jobs to try to make ends meet when he first developed an interest in apps.

Something about the app business intrigued him, yet nothing in his background indicated that he would be good at designing games or developing apps. David had worked as an army medic, a pool cleaner, a limo driver and at various other jobs when he first decided to learn about apps. Yet, David didn't let that stop him. Instead, he decided to jump with both feet right into his dream. He sold some video equipment he owned to finance the venture (and we're only talking about around $4,000), and he decided to learn how to make apps. Unfortunately, the first game he launched flopped. As did the second, the third... pretty much all of them up until app number 41. David's first 40 apps were all either total failures or marginal successes. From each one he learned something, and then kept going forward, *expecting* to eventually succeed.

Then he hit upon the multi-million-dollar idea. And that is where the key to it all lies. Somewhere deep inside himself David knew that he could be successful in this field if he could just figure out the right combination, and eventually that is exactly what happened. Now the rest is history, the app's audience is still growing and David and his team are working on new apps and games. Part of the reason I'm sharing this story is that David is very open about his dedication to practicing the principles of visualization, affirmations and positive thinking.

Those principles and practices helped him to develop a vision around his creation and, of course, led to great success. Without that vision, determination and dedication he certainly might have stopped chasing his dream long ago, and Color Switch might have never been developed.

What idea is bubbling up inside of you that simply cannot be kept down? If you're still reading this book perhaps you should take that as a sign that it's time to start listening to that voice and get ready to take some action to create that thing you've been thinking of. When you do so, do it with a conscious decision to expect things to work out in your favor. Does this mean that you should blindly follow an idea that is clearly never going to be lucrative? Well, no, not if you're looking to develop a viable business. But if you're truly passionate about something it might not need to be a million-dollar idea to bring you fulfillment and a life that you love. Someone I know has built a small business repairing old film cameras. His skills are very specialized, and he'll probably never get rich at what he does, but he loves getting up and heading over to his workshop every single morning, and that is worth something.

I believe that if you follow your true passion it will lead you to fulfillment and happiness. You should expect nothing less. Sure, you may need to return to the drawing board once or twice (or 40 times, like David did), but that is all part of the journey, part of the process.

If you're truly following a clear vision of something that you're feeling called to do then you don't really mind reinventing yourself a few times. Follow the passion. Be open to reinventing yourself, learning the lessons, and getting up and doing it all again. The worst thing you can do (and please, please, please don't do this...) is nothing. The worst thing is to hear the voice of your passion and your purpose and ignore it. Instead show up for life every day with your "game on" face. Show up and ask for guidance. Ask for life to be there for you. And expect nothing less.

When you do this, guess what?

You'll receive the very thing you wished for – the one you knew you'd be getting all along.

So, go right ahead and expect happiness, fulfillment and joy. Expect wealth and abundance. Expect anything else you're looking for out of life, then get ready to dig in and do the work.

It's time to find your grit and dig into your inner strength and determination. You've got this. It really is all there for the asking.

PAGE OF REFLECTION

Affirmation: *I expect to receive everything I've dreamed of. I know that life is always working in the interest of my higher self and higher purpose.*

Define the vision; what ARE you expecting? Describe your vision in great detail, using all your senses. What does it look like, smell like and taste like when you've achieved it?

What does happiness look like to you? Paint a picture, either using colored pencils, crayons or paints - or use your words - and describe this in great detail.

What old beliefs do you still need to let go of to make this happen for you?

What new ideas came up during these exercises?

PART 3
Grit

Grit is about showing up, doing the work and undertaking massive action.

Knock on a lot of doors. The right ones will always open, so it's just a matter of finding the resiliency to keep knocking.

In this resiliency are sown the seeds of success...

CHAPTER 9

What's Grit Got to Do With It?

"One characteristic emerged as a significant predictor of success. And it wasn't social intelligence. It wasn't good looks, physical health, and it wasn't IQ. It was grit."
- **Angela Lee Duckworth**, Professor of Psychology at University of Pennsylvania and leading researcher on "grit", from her TED Talk

What is grit, exactly? Who has it, and if you don't have it how then do you get it? In her TED Talk on the subject, Angela Lee Duckworth puts it eloquently: "Grit is passion and perseverance for very long-term goals. Grit is having stamina. Grit is sticking with your future, day in and day out, not just for the week. Not just for the month, but for years, and working really hard to make that future a reality. Grit is living life like it's a marathon, not a sprint."

Michelle Coleman Mayes, a bestselling author and accomplished lawyer, credits grit for helping her to climb the corporate ladder and for not allowing the inevitable stumbles to get in her way. She talks about grit that's born of failure by saying, "Without grit failure can drag you down. For example, I could have seen it as failure when a former boss did not select me for the deputy general counsel position at one of my former companies. I was disappointed, but I refused to relent just because he rejected me. I focused not on failure but on what counted: persistence, grit, perseverance, resilience... Failure is part of the journey."

GRIT is taking on the failure, the challenges and the struggles and keeping going with a relentless determination, a knowing that you can and will succeed.

When I think of the role models in my own life who exemplify grit I immediately think of my beautiful friend, Sylvia Gross. I met Sylvia when we lived just north of Los Angeles, in a unique and eclectic canyon community. The neighborhood was nestled in what are known as the foothills of the Angeles National Forest. The air is cleaner up there than it is in much of the rest of the city, but the heat is relentless and forest fires can ravage hundreds of square miles in a few short hours.

That canyon neighborhood was unlike anywhere I've lived before or since. I describe it by saying that we were all a bunch of misfits, brought together by chance, circumstance or, quite possibly, divine intervention. The terrain was wild and tough, with untamed brush, hot desert, plenty of lizards and the odd rattler. And the people fit right in - in that rough-and-tumble neighborhood, and with each other. We were a strangely functional extended family that was made up of an oddball bunch of actors, musicians, film industry professionals, teachers and municipal employees.

Despite how eclectic it was, or perhaps *because* we were all so different, the neighborhood was the most community-oriented, interesting and welcoming place I have ever lived. We were an island unto ourselves and even had our own traditions within the community. Our Greek neighbor, Yanni, was famous for his Easter lamb roasts and for his superhuman barbeque skills. Another neighbor opened up her home a couple of times each year for classical chamber music concerts, as several members of our community played with the various orchestras around town. The price of entry was a potluck dish and maybe a bottle of wine. Another neighbor built an actual amphitheater in her backyard and hosted concerts there for our collective enjoyment. It was an incredible time to be living in that place.

So, when developers threatened to come in and put more than 200 new homes right on our doorstep, no one was particularly happy about the prospect. The neighbors rallied, gathered, wrote letters and attended meetings, and in the course of all of that civic action we started hearing about a certain woman who could be our secret weapon in this fight – a brilliant lawyer and environmental activist named Sylvia, who also happened to live nearby.

Sylvia was an environmental lawyer who was known for her guts, her smarts and her savvy in navigating the system in situations like the one we found ourselves in. She was also in her 90's at the time we were fighting the developers but when she was asked if she could help there was no hesitation. Once she heard the details Sylvia was all-in.

As a participant in the ongoing organized protest against

the development I got to know Sylvia well. She advised our neighborhood group tirelessly and ended up commissioning me to help record her life story for the town historical society. It was a lucky turn of events and one that meant I was visiting her at least every week, recording the events of her remarkable life and of a woman who embodied the meaning of the word *grit.*

Sylvia was born just after the turn of the 20th century and when I was working with her she was nearly blind, approaching her 100th birthday, and still happily living in her canyon home with Jack, her faithful black lab. A fiercely independent woman, Sylvia cared for herself, swore like a sailor and I certainly wouldn't have wanted to get into a serious debate or argument with her because her mind was still as sharp as the proverbial tack.

Sylvia had lived a life of adventure, both in the States and abroad and, although it was not very common for women to work back then, Sylvia held professional positions from the time she was a teenager. She married twice, and was in her 50's when her second husband died. Although he left Sylvia comfortably well-off financially, she was never one to sit back and relax. She was going to fulfill a long-time dream and go to law school.

Never mind that there were precious few female lawyers back in the 1950's, when all of this transpired, or that middle-aged college students (particularly female ones) were practically unheard of. None of this deterred Sylvia because she had loads of grit, and if you have enough grit anything is possible. If you knew Sylvia you would know that no one was going to tell her that she couldn't do something once she had her mind set on it.

Sylvia eventually received her law degree at age 60 and went on to be hired by a prominent firm in Los Angeles. She worked there for years and continued to practice and consult up until nearly the end of her life. Sylvia embodied spunk, drive and determination, and that, dear readers, is what grit looks like.

It is a stubbornness, an unwillingness to give up. It is being met with obstacles, acknowledging them, then asking, "Yes, and...?" before moving on towards the goal, and she and all that she accomplished were nothing short of spectacular.

How and why should you apply the principles of grit to your own life?

We're all going to be faced with challenges of one kind or another, especially as we push ourselves outside of our comfort zone, to the place where we can build up some new part of our lives. There is no doubt that you will become intimately familiar with challenges of one kind or another as you journey towards your goals and your dreams. There will be days when you easily handle the bumps in the road, and there will be other times when everything feels so hard that you won't even want to get out of bed in the morning.

The thing to remember is, many of the things that are stressing you out at any given time are going to be non-issues in a month or a year. A little perspective can go a long way when you're looking for your grit. I'll share with you one of my tricks. It involves allowing yourself to believe in the possibility that there is a solution to your problem. You don't need to know how this solution is going to appear; you just need to know (and truly believe) that it will come. Then, you commit to showing up day in and day out.

You ignore the naysayers and knock on lots of doors, knowing that eventually the right ones will start opening up. Sometimes it helps to get really clear on what the end game looks like, and to commit to doing your best to inch towards that goal every single day. Plenty of days you might not think you're moving the needle at all, but persevere and eventually momentum will build, until the day when you tip the scale and the floodgates open.

Sometimes, if you are a trailblazer like Sylvia, the obstacles that you face will be significant. Other times your challenges may be smaller and more mundane, but even mundane problems can feel insurmountable at times. Having and developing your grit muscles means that you don't give up. You persevere. You show up again and again and keep your focus on whatever it is that you're working to achieve. That focus is critically important because it will become your beacon of light when times get tough.

I had no idea what I was made of until the going got tough...

My own grit showed up in a big way when my business was at one of its lowest points. Sales had been in a decline for months, despite all our efforts with marketing our services, and expenses were significantly higher than revenues. Those expenses were largely made up of employee salaries, and when cash flow was bad, I even took on a sizable debt to try to keep the business going.

The business model was clearly unsustainable, but at the time I felt paralyzed by fear; unable to take the action that was needed. Everything I owned was tied up in that business, not to mention all of the blood, sweat and tears that I had invested over the years. I cared deeply about the business and the employees. In addition, my family depended on the income that was the sole source for covering our own living expenses.

Here is where I wish I could tell you that I dug my heels in and with superhuman grit and determination turned the business around. That did actually happen, but not exactly at the speed at which I wanted or needed it to. In my case things had to get worse before they got better. If the business did not exactly collapse, it at least stumbled and suffered a pretty bad fall. Eventually, I had to do the very thing I was most terrified of; namely, letting the employees go. That time in my life was horrible on so many levels, but there was also a whisper of relief, of no longer having the responsibility of struggling to make payroll while going through the restructuring process.

It was dark and painful and sad, but there is something about hitting rock bottom that can lead to new life, and in my case, that's what happened. When everything fell apart it was devastating but I didn't have the luxury of staying in a place of panic and despair for too long. I had no choice but to figure out how to make things work, and sometimes when there are no other options that's when your grit really gets to show off and do its thing.

For me the whole grit thing took a while. First, I wanted to crawl into a hole. Then, I just wanted to hide with the covers over my head. There were tears, sickening moments of full-on terror and regret, but then one day things began to shift ever so slightly, and grit finally started showing up. It was very quiet at first – so quiet I hardly noticed it was in the room. Then it grew bigger and "badder" and before you knew it, I was in the zone.

I was going to survive, dammit.

And so was some version of my business because I and everyone else had given too much for too long to just let the whole thing go without a fight. Sure, it would be a different business than it was before, but as I started to envision and believe in a new reality, things began to turn around.

As with many such tragedies, the collapse of my business actually created an opportunity for reinvention, and for a totally new business model. Going through the transition was breathtakingly painful for me and everyone else who was involved, but there was also a kind of beauty in the process, as well. For me, I needed to surrender to the fact that I didn't have all the answers, and that I would need to go within for guidance and support. A lot of soul searching ensued, but what resulted from all of that was the idea that I could take all the lessons learned and create something different. I finally began to see that I could help other people who were going through similar struggles, and that's the moment that a whole new journey began.

To me, grit is about showing up. It's about getting knocked down and bringing your best effort forward again and again. Grit is taking back your own power. It's hearing what others are saying yet choosing to believe (and acting upon) your own intuition. It's not about staying on the same path you have been journeying on, unless that's what your truth calls you to do. There's no victory in beating a dead horse, so to speak. Sometimes you will get knocked flat on your back, and it's in the getting up that the grit comes in. In my case changing direction in my business was undoubtedly the right thing to do. As soon as I made the decision to restructure, new clients started showing up, and the work they were bringing was much more in line with the type of projects that I really enjoy. I also had to do some soul-searching to make sure my talents and interests were aligned with my own job description.

In the midst of all of this, I also started writing, as honestly and openly as I could, and I began publishing my articles online. I didn't know whether any of it would come to anything, but people actually read what I wrote, and I began to get thank you comments and emails, and sometimes even calls, from people all over the US, and in a few foreign countries as well. These notes bolstered my spirits immensely, and a lot of times on the toughest of days I'd get a call or a note from somebody who told me that one of my articles really helped them or I'd see that one of my articles was shared and got lots of hits. I tried to remember to celebrate those little victories and to take them as confirmation that I was on the right path. Even when I got that scathing review from someone in Australia, I celebrated. I wasn't thrilled to be criticized, obviously, but on the other hand my post had reached a complete stranger all the way across the world, and he cared enough to take the time to respond. To me, even this experience was an affirmation that I should be doing more writing, which is something that I never seemed to have time or energy to do before. It's true that there always is a silver lining, another way forward, but only if you continue to get up and show up, and that is what grit is all about.

The Beauty of Struggle

Over the years my biggest lesson around grit has been to take the worry, challenges, success and failure and embrace it all. Embrace the good and the bad and realize that everything that happens – *everything* – is a learning opportunity. Change, whether you label it as "good" or "bad", always brings opportunity along with it, in one form or another.

You know what else brings on the opportunities? The tough, unpleasant times. The really uncomfortable places where we all must go, at one point or another. And all the stuff that no one ever wants to deal with or experience. The trials all leave you more flexible, with gumption, wisdom and hard-earned perspective. No one ever gets these things when times are good and easy. Character and grit both get brought out for exercise when life is dark, bleak and scary.

They also come out when people tell you that you can't do something, or when they try to put barriers in your way. My friend Sylvia faced animosity from classmates and professors when she decided to go to law school when she was well into middle age, and a woman to boot! It would have been much easier for her to give up and to have a nice, quiet life for the rest of her years. But that was not who she was, and the very fiber of what she was made of would never have allowed her to do that. And you know what? The more you develop your own grit the less likely you're going to be able to sit on the sidelines, either.

It all starts with that one time you get knocked down and don't stay there. Then you do it again and again. You march forward with your eye firmly fixed on the destination, and you just keep going, despite the storms, despite the inevitable detours. You keep going forward with your grit, on this road of life.

PAGE OF REFLECTION

Affirmation: *I have plenty of grit and determination to make my dreams come true.*

Think about a time in your life when you used your grit to get something difficult done. Describe it. How were you feeling going through that? How did you feel afterwards?

When you know and trust that you have all the grit you need to carry you through any circumstance it gives you a sense of empowerment and invincibility. What are some other words that come to mind when you think of wearing an imaginary armor of grit and fortitude?

What new ideas came up during these exercises?

CHAPTER 10
And... Action

*The path to success is to take massive,
determined actions.*
- **Tony Robbins**

Action is the foundational key to all success.
- **Pablo Picasso**

*You don't have to be great to start but you have
to start to be great.*
- **Zig Ziglar**

This might be the most important chapter in this whole book. In fact, in one way or another everything has been leading up to this point, to the place where you're going to start doing something about actually achieving your dream. And that is exciting. It's real. It's big, and of all the things we talk about in this book this is the chapter that is going to most directly affect the level of your success.

You can do all the preparation in the world, you can clear out your thoughts and you can flex your grit muscles, but if you're not willing to get up and show up and do what needs to be done then there is simply no way you're going to be able to make the kind of progress that is going to be required to create the life you've been dreaming of.

And here is where the life dance begins – that delicate balance between holding tight to your "end game" vision, stepping forward with courage and faith and physically taking the steps that will make the difference. Which leads us to the very big and all-important question: where to start?

For me, I am a list maker, so that's how I'm going to talk about this methodology. If you are a more tactile or visual person, feel free to work through these exercises by putting your own special spin to them. Some people who are more visual need to draw out a chart or diagram. Others work with a giant pile of sticky notes and an empty wall, literally plotting out a course of action. Others create a linear vision board with pictures that symbolize milestones that they plan to achieve along the way. Whatever your preferred method, you'll need some means of writing down a lot of ideas and you'll also need a calendar.

Step One: No limits

First of all, you have to write down *all* the things you can think of that you would ideally want and/or need in order to start your business (or other new endeavor). This is probably going to be a VERY long list, and it might even take you several days or weeks to complete. On this list do not allow yourself to be at all limited by your own reality. Your present circumstances have no bearing on your future success, so if you catch yourself saying something like, "But I have no idea how to do that" or "I don't have enough money for that," kindly ask those voices to be quiet and get back to the task at hand. Let me show you what I mean.

For example, imagine that I want to open a retail store that sells plants and gardening tools.

My list might include things like: I need a business license, a retail space, some land on which I can grow my own plants, connections to suppliers, staff to help me run my business, a logo and branding, marketing and advertising, displays, signage, a website, merchandise, cash registers, a bank account, customers... etc.

Again, if you feel that something should be on the list, do not leave it off for "practical" reasons. If you feel that you need a retail space – even if you don't have a single penny in the bank or means to get that space right now, *put it on the list.*

Try to think of all the details, and if you have a few trusted friends that you can run this list by, go ahead and do so because chances are that they may think of other things that you haven't considered. Do you need a business permit or some other kind of certification? Do you need to get a sales tax number? Some kind of special training? Whatever comes to mind, put it on the list.

BRAINSTORM

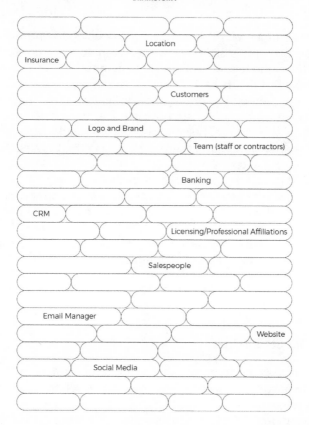

Location

Insurance

Customers

Logo and Brand

Team (staff or contractors)

Banking

CRM

Licensing/Professional Affiliations

Salespeople

Email Manager

Website

Social Media

So, now how are you feeling?

Are you a little overwhelmed or scared? Are those negative thoughts starting to creep back in – thoughts like, "This is too much, I'll never be able to do this" or "This is such a crazy dream... I need to just let it go now"?

The purpose of the exercise is not to discourage you. Rather, it is intended to wake up your scrappy, gritty self – the one who says, "Hell yes, I can do this!"

As we continue with this chapter you're going to end up with a real, comprehensible and smart plan to get you started. And throughout it all, you must remember one of the basic principles of this book: The Universe is there to support you along this journey. You do NOT have to figure out the "how" part of every item on your list, and you certainly don't have to tackle them all at one time, but it is critically important that you do write them down. Claim them as yours. Let the Universe know in no uncertain terms that this is the direction you're headed in, and that this is what you're building ("this or something better"). Then know that as you continue on this journey and show up to do the work, you'll also be given gifts in the form of lucky breaks and so-called coincidences. In order to receive these gifts you do need to show up with 100% commitment, which means getting into action around your big dream.

Are you still with me? Okay, let's take a deep breath and keep going.

Step Two: Get Organized

Now we're going to go back to your master list and split it up into two groups: those things that you absolutely, positively need to get started on creating this big dream, and the things that would be "nice" to have. If you've done your list on sticky notes it will be easy to separate out items. If you've written the list out, you may need to rewrite everything here, but trust me. This is part of the process and it's extremely important. Plus, every time you write out your "wish list" it's another affirmation to yourself and to the Universe that you're really serious about this thing. And besides, you've got grit. You can handle this!

So, now, once you've got your two lists let's focus first on the "needs" one. Once you've got all of those "needs" together in one place, rewrite the list one more time, ranking the needs in order of importance. If it's a long list, then pick out the top 10 things and use those to continue with this exercise. You can go back and add the others later, and you can also apply this same treatment to your "wants", but let's start with the things that are going to have the biggest impact on a positive outcome.

Once you've got your 10 most important "must-haves" you'll need to put those into a chart that looks like this:

"Must Have" Item	Resources I have	Resources I need	Action step

The "Needs" can be anything that is required to start your endeavor. Think about technology, physical space, professional resources, human resources, customers, and financial considerations, etc. Remember, when you are first starting out you might not be able to afford top-of-the-line equipment or other items. Figure out which items you really need and then get creative about where you find them. For example, maybe you can't afford a brand new computer, but could start out with a second hand older model.

The "Resources" columns are there to help you identify the people, knowledge, certifications, connections and other assets that will be valuable to you as you look to grow your business. If you already have access to those resources, then what action step do you need to take to put that item into play?

If you do not currently have the right connections, knowledge, capital or platform then how can you find out more about that thing that you're missing? What calls can you make, what research can you do and how can you talk to the people who know more than you do about this subject? Reach out to them and start asking the questions. See who else they can put you in touch with.

As you do this, you'll find that most people are willing to help you out if you just ask. Also, the more you put yourself out there and start talking about your dream with confidence that you are going to achieve it, the more you're going to find "random" people showing up to help you. You may not get help from every person you talk to, but the right ones will appear. You just have to keep asking the questions and keep coming back with that sheer determination that you will ultimately succeed.

I'm getting information but I still don't know how to start my business.

You still don't have to be bothered by knowing the exact steps of how you're going to achieve your goals; you just have to know what your goals are and start the whole thing in motion by getting into action and getting on the path. Little by little, you will get there, as long as you **trust the process and don't stop moving forward**.

A friend of mine dreams of opening a resort in Costa Rica. While there is a significant gap of knowledge, capital and other resources between where she is now and where she wants to be, one of her initial steps involved researching the real estate market in Costa Rica and making some fact-finding trips to the region. She doesn't have her resort yet, but she recently bought a property there and is in the initial stages of building a house. The step by step details of how it's all going to work out are not clear, but that really doesn't matter. She's showing up with a request to the Universe and a commitment to moving forward with an open heart and mind. I have no doubt that she will get to own or run a resort there one day – or end up doing something even better.

Sometimes when you go through this exercise you start to get some creative ideas about how you can start to make things happen. And, while this chapter is geared towards starting a business, you can use the same technique for other things, as well.

I was working with someone who lives on the east coast but who wanted to spend six months of the year in California visiting friends and family. When she came to me she thought that her dream was impossible. She is retired and lives within a very strict budget. Spending half the year in California seemed like something only rich people could do – until we started talking and I encouraged her to do the chart exercise.

As she began breaking down the steps one of the things that occurred to her was that she might be able to sublet her current apartment, and moreover, based on current AirBNB prices, she might even make enough money to subsidize her trip. Further investigation revealed an opportunity to stay with someone who was looking for a part time companion for an elderly woman, and this suddenly meant that the expensive housing she thought she couldn't afford was now taken care of. The deeper my client got into this process the clearer the path became and, ultimately, she was able to do that thing she had always dreamed of and spend part of the year on the west coast. Certainly, there were many pieces that did have to fall into place before that happened, but by creating the chart you can start to view your action steps in achievable chunks, rather than as an insurmountable (and ill-defined) challenge.

The power of the resources chart is that it helps to shift your thinking from focusing on all the reasons that you can't do something, and brings the power back to what you can do. No matter where you are starting from there are resources, people, connections and more you can access today. And this could mean starting out at the public library with the librarian as your first source of knowledge, but that works too. Wherever you're starting from, the biggest key is to just do it.

Which brings me to the next step in the process...

Step Three: Set Your To-do's

Once you have your resource map done for at least your top 10 things, you now have to translate that information into an actionable to-do list. I recommend that you carve out time *every single day* to continue working on turning your dream into a reality. This means that you have to make the commitment to yourself that you're going to set aside time to do this, and that you're going to fiercely protect this time from anyone and everyone who tries to pull you away.

A time management tip for you is, an hour spent on pushing your big dream forward is worth more than eight hours doing "busy" work. If you want to make big changes in your life, and if you want to see results from those changes fast, then get serious about filling up your list with those little things that are going to add up to big results and take the time to do something meaningful. Every. Single. Day.

Now that you understand the importance of this commitment you can get your calendar out and start setting up tasks for yourself to complete each day. You probably only want to schedule a week or two at a time because once you start taking action and talking with different people you may be sent in new and unexpected directions based on the advice you get. The key is to keep the momentum up by doing something, anything, daily.

Step Four: Set Milestones

This is another calendar task, and you want to make sure that you can somehow print out these milestones or post them up on a wall so that you can see them every day. You also want to be able to edit them and replace these initial goals with new ones. Why would this be important? Because every time you achieve one of them, you'll have to mark it as complete and set a new goal for yourself to take its place.

Building dreams, business, and life means that once you achieve one goal you pause, you acknowledge your accomplishment, and then you change the goalposts and aim for something new. You're never going to find that you've "arrived" and have nothing else to strive for. After all, life is all about the journey, and that's what keeps it interesting.

So, pick 5-10 milestones or goals that you would like to achieve as part of your journey, and mark them down on the calendar on the dates that you plan to accomplish them by. When you get into action around your dream, you're actually going to be surprised by how quickly some of these goals turn into reality, but to start with, just put them down on the calendar on dates that seem to make sense to you. If you miss your own deadlines, go ahead and revise them. This exercise is not intended to add guilt or stress to your life, but it is designed to move you into action.

Notable milestones might include having a conversation with someone who might be difficult to get in touch with, buying or leasing a property, or registering a business name. It might mean securing funding, hiring a business coach or hitting certain sales numbers. Pick milestones that make sense and are meaningful to you, write them down, and again, don't worry too much about how you're going to achieve them.

Milestone I am Striving For	Date by Which I'll Achieve This Goal	Completed

Milestone I am Striving For	Date by Which I'll Achieve This Goal	Completed

As you continue to take action during the coming weeks and months you will find yourself inspired by new action steps that you will add to your list, and before you know it you will achieve your goals as long as you keep going forward. And of course, this chapter appears in the grit section of the book for this very reason: you must keep going with sheer determination.

Sheer determination and one last thing...

Step Five: Prepare to Dance

The final thing to mention in this "action" chapter is how important flexibility is. This is not to say that your goals have to keep changing or that you should take your eyes off of the prize, but you must stay open to guidance from the Universe and be willing to tweak the direction you're going in. Why is this? Because there may, in fact, be a quicker and better way to get there than the one that you originally laid out in your first road map. You must give yourself permission to adjust course along the way because that is where the magic and adventure happens. It's also where you often find out that the Universe has something much greater in store for you than you ever could have imagined.

Remember, at every point of your journey you always make the best decisions possible based on your knowledge, abilities and resources up until that point. You plan out your steps to the best of your ability, however, as you go along you are going to be introduced to new opportunities that you could never have predicted back at the beginning. That's why we talk about this journey being like a dance. It's a delicate balance of planning and following your inner and outer guidance. It's a game of being open to opportunities and to learning how to identify and evaluate them as they come up for you.

The more you practice, the better you'll get at identifying which opportunities are worth pursuing and which ones are more of a red herring. You'll most likely make some mistakes along the way, but that's when you dig deep and draw upon your grit, determination and your undying drive to keep going, onto more adventures and opportunities along the way.

And that, my friend, is where life's magic truly shines and where you realize that it all really was worth every minute that you put into the building of your dream.

PAGE OF REFLECTION

Affirmation: *All it takes is baby steps moving in the right direction. I don't have to understand the "how".*

What are some action steps you commit to taking in pursuit of your business or your dream? When will you complete those by?

What other thoughts came up for you as you work through these exercises?

CHAPTER 11
Knocking on Heaven's Door

What we really want to do is what we are really meant to do. When we do what we are meant to do, money comes to us, doors open for us, we feel useful, and the work we do feels like play to us.
-**Julia Cameron**

Everybody dies, but not everybody lives.
-**Prince Ea**

Have you had your defining moment yet? You know the one. That pivotal time when you draw your line in the sand, state loud and clear what you're here for and when you finally decide to stop wasting time on other people's drama and bullshit. In your defining moment, you make the decision to stop playing small, stop making excuses and step up to take center stage in your own life. It's when you decide once and for all that *you're doing this thing you've been called to do all this time*.

For some of us this moment isn't a moment at all, but instead it's something that happens over time. We begin to realize that we are actively designing our own life. We have a choice of who we spend our time engaging with and where we're focusing our energy. We begin to develop a clearer picture of what it is we really want out of life and we begin to make adjustments – perhaps just small ones at first – that bring us into alignment with our passion and our purpose. This shift can take weeks or months or even years for some people, and if you're one of those people, don't worry. A slow evolution leads you to the same place and is just as powerful as a dramatic defining moment.

For others this shift really is something that happens in the blink of an eye. It comes in the wake of the diagnosis of a serious illness, the death of a loved one, or a tragedy somewhere in the world. Whatever it is, once this thing happens, we, ourselves, are never the same again. We're forever changed because we've glimpsed one of life's biggest truths – the one that reveals to us that we're not here on earth to suffer, but instead to thrive and prosper and to live out our own destiny. And here's the kicker: the clock is always ticking. We all get a limited time in this game and the moment you *really know* that, everything changes.

And get ready, because whether you're aware of it or not, this shift is already beginning to happen to you. Just by reading this book you've put something wonderful into motion. The things you now know can't be unlearned and your journey has already begun. The trick is, you have to decide whether you're going to keep moving forward or if you're going to stick with the way you've always done things.

The other day I had lunch with a friend who is in remission from a rare and particularly nasty form of esophageal cancer. Her pivotal moment came with the first diagnosis several years ago. The rebirth, awakening and feeling like she had been given a second chance all happened more recently, when the doctors announced she was in remission. Yet, that good news came with a caveat. If she gets through the next two years, there is a quite good chance the cancer will stay away long-term. But those two years bring with them a high risk that the disease will re-emerge with a new ferocity, and this constant reminder of her own mortality has changed everything for her.

So, how do you think this friend spends her time? I'd be lying if I said that she never thinks about the cancer, but she certainly doesn't focus on it. Instead she does her best to eat and live healthy, to laugh a lot and to be choosy about who she hangs out with. She no longer cares much about money and material belongings, but she does seek out satisfaction and enriching experiences for herself. In this friend's case, teaching her craft, which happens to be writing, brings her a lot of joy, as does volunteering for causes she believes in.

I was recently talking to another friend who is caring for her ill mother. I asked her how she was handling things and she laughed. "Well," she said, "I'm juggling a lot. I still have to work, and Mom needs a lot right now, which is my priority. But now I'm less inclined than ever before to get sucked into other people's demands or drama. I always ask myself if something is really going to matter in five minutes, five days, five weeks or five years. If the answer is no, I just let it go. And for 95% of the time the answer is that it won't matter at all, so I let it go."

How Living Like You're Dying
Helps You Create Your Dream Life

Part One: Protect Your Peace

I love the wisdom in the two stories above because both of them demonstrate how you can quickly get to a place of knowing for certain what your priorities should be. And once you do that, it is a lot easier to say no to things that don't serve you. Boundaries are important for all sorts of reasons. They keep you out of other people's drama and prevent you from playing the game of life by rules that are made up by other people.

How do you do this, given the demands of everyday life? One of the best ways is to hit the "pause" button. Instead of reacting immediately the next time someone provokes you, or demands that you do something, just wait. Breathe. Count backwards from 15. And consider what reaction (if any) is warranted. When you start practicing this you'll find a new sense of peace and freedom.

The pause also helps protect you from your own "worst case scenario stories" that can come up in your mind as you face conflict or challenges. And, believe it or not, the pause can also help you grow your grit muscle. Remember that grit means that you're in it for the long haul, and if you're always reacting to things you're not conserving your energy or spending it wisely.

The pause brings you back to a place of power. Learn to slow down, stay laser focused and embrace that all-powerful two-lettered word: NO.

There is freedom waiting for you
On the breezes of the sky
And you ask, "What if I fall?"
Oh, but my darling, what if you fly?
-Erin Hanson

Part Two: Your Time to Shine

Here is where I challenge you to take everything next level. There is no doubt that it's critical to learn how to play defense. You *absolutely* must protect your sacred space, your mind, your time and your focus. To truly win at life, you also must learn to excel at offense. That means you have to go out, actively chase your dreams then take steps to bring them to fruition.

Does that sound overwhelming? Many people never end up taking any action at all because they get frustrated or scared when they realize they can't see the whole path in front of them. The unknown is certainly disconcerting for many of us, but a big part of life is not being able to know anything for sure, so the sooner you get comfortable with that, the better.

It is never important to figure out every single step between where you are now and where you need to be to be living the life of your dreams. In fact, trying to map this out in detail is actually impossible because you cannot possibly predict all of the situations that are going to come up along the way. By all means lay out a strategy for yourself but know that it's going to change countless times as you venture forth on your journey.

But don't worry. View life as a grand adventure and you'll find that you're embracing the unknown. The things that you can never predict are the very elements that make the game of life so much fun. For example, you might set up a launch event for your product (*taking action*) and maybe you make some sales. Then someone that you randomly get introduced to turns out to be a journalist and does a feature piece on you (*coincidence, serendipity*). That bit of press, which you neither solicited nor paid for, could be the one thing that changes everything (*your life miracle*).

The very scenario that I described above actually happened to a friend of mine who now has a thriving company, but who, prior to that, struggled for years. His company seemed to be continually teetering on the financial edge, and several times he was on the verge of giving up. My friend and his employees knew they had a great product, but while they tried all sorts of things to become profitable, they never could reach the sales numbers they needed. Then one day they made it into the national news when a journalist wrote a feature article about their product. Soon, other newspapers and TV shows also ran the story, and orders came flooding in, giving them the boost they so badly needed. The rest, as they say, is history.

The only reason that my friend's company got to the point where he got that press was because while he definitely did consider the possibility of giving up, he didn't do that. Instead he dug deeper and found the resolve to carry on. And if you're going to go into business for yourself I can promise you that the day will come when you'll have to tap into your own grit in order to get through some tough times. In fact, "grit" stories are so prevalent among successful businesses that I would venture to say that is probably one of the main common denominators of all of them.

Another friend of mine, Megan Murphy, has an interesting story about grit. Several years ago she started a strange little hobby where she would paint inspirational messages on rocks and drop them in random places for strangers to find. It didn't take very long for Megan's rocks to make their way around the world, and for her odd habit to become a movement. Megan got the idea to write a book about her experience and was rejected by publisher after publisher. Fast-forward a few months, and Oprah featured Megan and her Kindness Rocks Project in her magazine. Now, with a new level of media attention, publishers that wouldn't talk to Megan a few months ago are suddenly giving her another look.

You just never know where your "big break" is going to come from or when this is going to happen. You just have to keep showing up.

Stay focused on your goal and on taking the steps you need to take to get there, but stay open to miracles along the way, too, because those are the things that are going to propel you forward in unimaginable and wonderful ways.

Son, if you really want something in life you have to work for it. Now quiet! They're about to announce the lottery numbers.
-Homer Simpson

Part Three: Live Like a Lottery Winner

Who hasn't fantasized about winning the lottery? You buy a ticket, your numbers are called and all of a sudden you have more money than you could imagine and overnight you're thrust into a world of luxury.

The unfortunate truth is that most lottery winners don't actually end up living happily ever after. In fact, the stories of broken friendships and families are many and the vast majority of major lottery winners (more than 70%) are broke again within seven years.

What if you really could have the good parts of your fantasy lifestyle without the downside? What if I could convince you to start doing this today? Would you say yes to some of the things you're dreaming about or will you continue denying yourself?

As you journey forward towards making your dreams come true, part of the secret to success is acting as if you've already got many of the things you want. This seems like a contradiction but it actually is very possible, especially when you start experiencing some of the things you imagine in your fantasy dream life.

Several years ago, I lived across the street from a young family and became friendly with Beth, the mom. We both had young children at the time and enjoyed spending time together doing crafts and taking the kids on little field trips. Then one day, out of the blue, Beth announced that they were moving to Santa Cruz. I needed to know all the details. Did her husband have a job there? Did they have family there? What were they going to do?

Well, as it turned out they did have a couple of leads on jobs, but nothing was definite at the time they made the decision to move. They also hadn't won the actual lottery, but Beth explained to me that they had decided to stop waiting to live the lottery to live their dreams. They had always wanted to move to Santa Cruz and figured that there was no time like the present.

Was this a bold move? Absolutely. Was there the risk of failure? Of course. Did they step right into their dream house and not have any challenges along the way? No, of course not. But they did take a big action towards their dream and are today living a happy and prosperous life in Santa Cruz. In my book that is about a million times better than dreaming about something and never taking action towards it.

If there is something you're dreaming of, find a way to do it now. Do you want to own your own sailing boat someday? Even if you can't afford to buy a boat today, you can start hanging around the marina and getting to know other boat owners. There are plenty of people who do own boats who would love to have you come out and sail with them to keep them company. Take action today to get you closer to your big dream and start living as if you really have won the lottery.

Another way to start experiencing prosperity is to stop saying things like, "I can't afford that" or "That's way too expensive for me."

Those statements do not support you as you mold and craft the life of your dreams. I'm not suggesting that you should blindly and foolishly spend money you don't have, but try this phrase instead: "Let's figure out how we can make that work."

Besides watching your language, I also suggest that you find ways to treat yourself from time as a way to feel and experience abundance. It's important to do this to train yourself to believe that abundance is your default state. As you're retraining your brain in this way, allow yourself to be guilt-free and joyful in whatever splurge you are indulging in, whether it be a massage at a spa, an expensive piece of chocolate or a weekend getaway.

Feel the gratitude, soak in the abundance and know that you are already wealthy beyond compare. Know this with every ounce of your being, and so it shall be.

> *You can have anything you want in life*
> *if you're willing to give up the belief that you can't*
> *have it.*
> **-Robert Anthony**

Part 4: Pick Your Prize

Here is the most serious and most important point in this whole book: Now that you have been handed the keys to the kingdom what are you waiting for?

I hope that you're now convinced that if you can dream it you can do it, so why not start today to create the life you really want for yourself? Do I need to tell you again that your time here on Earth is limited, finite, and is quickly running out?

The reality is, you can create anything in this life that you desire, but first you must have a clear picture of what your end game is. Then you need to believe that achieving it is possible, and finally you must commit to steadfast determination and promise yourself that you're in the journey for the long haul.

This is what they call the "leap of faith", when you imagine something and just believe so deeply that it's possible that you take a chance on yourself. And, really, who better to take a gamble on than you? So, lean into your dream. Imagine it, feel it and then start living it. Anything you want in life really is available to you.

What is stopping you from reaching out and grabbing all that you've been dreaming of?

It's all here, yours for the asking. So, what are you waiting for?

PAGE OF REFLECTION

Affirmation: *I have the right and responsibility to create a magical, fulfilling and full life both for myself and for those around me.*

Can you commit to one ritual for starting each day and for ending each day? This can be something very simple but should ground you and remind you of your power and your purpose. It should bring you back to your gratitude and joy. Describe your ritual.

Create a simple one-page business plan and a one-page life plan. Focus on the areas listed and write words, phrases and action steps that will keep you focused in each of your key areas.

What new ideas come up during these exercises?

BUSINESS PLAN

What
What we do (the problem we solve)
Differentiators (what makes us unique)

Who
Customers (who we do it for) → Persona

Who do you need on your core team?		Who are your trusted advisors?
Role	Name	Accountant - Lawyer - Coach - Mentors - Trusted Peer Group -

Who are your competitors? (Name at least top 3-5)

Awareness	
Marketing (getting your business known) ☐ Community Involvement ☐ Press/Earned Media ☐ Social Media	Advertising (paid placement) ☐ SEO Plan ☐ Paid Digital ☐ Traditional

Financials	
Funding your business - sources: ☐ Self fund ☐ Investors ☐ Loans ☐ Grants	How much will you need and how will you get it?

How much money do you need to make monthly to break even? To profit?
How are you pricing your items/packages?
How many items/packages will you have to sell?

Legacy
The best businesses contrinute to their communities.   What do you want to be known for? How will you give back?

LIFE PLAN

What I Have	What I Want	3 Action Steps
Health		1 2 3
Money		1 2 3
Business/Work		1 2 3
Friends & Family		1 2 3
Romance/Life Partner		1 2 3
Home & Environment		1 2 3
Fun & Hobbies		1 2 3
Legacy/Giving Back		1 2 3

AN INVITATION

Thank you for joining me to learn about the Ready, Set, Grit process. I hope that you've found a new way of thinking and of getting into action so you truly can turn your dreams into reality.

But because being part of a group of like-minded individuals vastly stacks the odds of success in your favor, I'd like to invite you to join our growing community of entrepreneurs, thought leaders and game changers.

You'll find resources to help you along your journey, as well as invitations to receive group or individual coaching and a peer community that wants to help you succeed.

Please visit elinbarton.com for more information.

I look forward to seeing you there!

Very best,

Elin

ACKNOWLEDGEMENTS

Thank you for reading this book. I hope you enjoyed it and were able to get some useful information and action steps from it.

Until I fully immersed myself in the process of writing I never realized how much of a community effort producing a book would be. I had always thought of writers as solitary creatures – introverts who drink a lot of coffee and wine and who ruminate quietly on the state of the world. What I found to be the reality of it, however, was a completely different story. There is a whole team of people who have to share the credit for bringing this book to life, and I'm certain that I'm forgetting to list some of them here. Please forgive my unintentional oversight.

First and foremost, I have to thank my husband, John. He is my first reader and can always be counted on to ask the right questions and to give honest and well thought out feedback. Without him asking those tough questions and his determination to steer me away from taking the easy way out, this would have been a much-diminished piece of work.

Then there is Sean Patrick, my publisher and founder of That Guy's House. We came into each other's life at just the right time – his first year as a publisher and my first time as an author. From the start we shared a vision and a passion and have shaped this book together. The book didn't come out that first year or the year after, but Sean and I both knew enough to understand that it would be birthed at the very right time, and so it was. For that I am deeply grateful.

I am lucky enough to have other friends in the publishing business who were kind and generous, and who provided unwavering support, encouragement and advice. Laura Ponticello deserves the highest thanks for the generosity of her time and for her valuable guidance and advice. I treasure the memories of our lunches, Laura, and we must find another project so we can continue them.

Ellyn Sanna is another book publisher who went so far above and beyond what I ever hoped for, by not only tirelessly answering my many questions about writing, publishing and cover design, but also for providing valuable insight into industry trends and best practices. I appreciate the clear and honest feedback and all the ways that she helped to make this a much better and more powerful book.

Many of my friends have read early drafts of the book and provided valuable suggestions and feedback, but no one has been as consistent and loyal as my friend, Christine Day. Christine is one of my best readers, proofreaders and editors, all in one beautiful package. I'm proud to call her my friend and am honored beyond words that she has been such a willing participant in the process of putting this book together.

Bonni Phelps and I created our own little mastermind and offered support to one another's entrepreneurial efforts. Those sessions may have sometimes involved snacks from Baked Euphoria and wine from Antonio's and they definitely led directly to the coining of this book's title. Thank you, my friend!

Then there is my amazing community of treasured business coaches and advisers, my friends and colleagues, and of course, my entrepreneurial peeps – the Goldman Sachs community and members of I.C. Genius and The Boardroom, in particular. You guys are amazing, and the encouragement, feedback and suggestions you have offered has been invaluable. Thank you for following me and for helping to drive this whole movement.

And last but certainly not least, there's my family. My beautiful daughters, Zoe and Sophie, were steadfast in their belief that this book needed to be written. My parents, aunts, uncles, cousins... all of the people that kept asking about the book and encouraging me so much that there was no way I couldn't finish it!

This truly was a dream come true, and you were all a valuable piece of making this happen.

To everyone who supported turning this very big dream into a reality, I thank you and appreciate you all from the bottom of my heart.

ABOUT THE AUTHOR

An entrepreneurial leader, success coach and motivational speaker, Elin Barton empowers others to achieve their dreams and transform their lives.

Elin is committed to breaking down barriers of geography with her online communities that provide support and continuous education and development for business owners and leaders. If you are interested in learning more about these communities, and other offers and upcoming events, please visit elinbarton.com.

When she is not traveling, Elin enjoys her home in Upstate New York where she can often be found gardening, cooking and going on long walks with her dogs and husband, John.